Student's Book 1

PETER VINEY AND KAREN VINEY

Oxford University Press 1989

Note on recorded material:

All presentation material is recorded except in Units 7, 11, 12, and 40.

listening development activities

songs

The recordings occur on the cassette in the order in which they appear in the Student's Book units.

Teachers are reminded that if they do not wish students to write in their books, answers should be written on a separate sheet of paper.

Contents

Introduction English words

1 Fasten seat belts

2 Self-service

3 Is it a star?

4 Names and addresses

5 Lambert and Stacey

6 The London train

7 Space station

8 What's it like?

9 Where is she?

10 Quiz of the Week

11 Is there any . . .?

12 The Family

13 People

14 How much is it?

15 The Keys

Story for pleasure: Security

16 Directions

17 Marchmain Castle

18 It's mine!

19 Asking for things

20 Chips with everything

21 Mickey can't dance

22 What time . . .?

23 Flight 201

24 Comet!

25 K Division Metro Police

Story for pleasure: The Secret of the Pyramid

26 The weather

27 She doesn't like interviews

28 Wants and needs

29 Regular hours?

30 A day in the life of Dennis Cook

Story for pleasure: The Third Planet

31 The outback

32 Tracey's first day

33 Beware of pickpockets!

34 A good dinner

35 One dark night

Story for pleasure: Crocodile Preston

36 The Morgans

37 Having a conversation

38 Going home

39 Offers and suggestions

40 Treasure Island

Irregular verbs

Listening appendix

Vocabulary index

Grammar summaries

English words

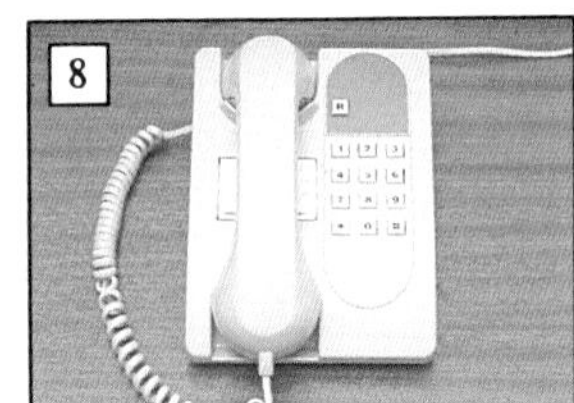

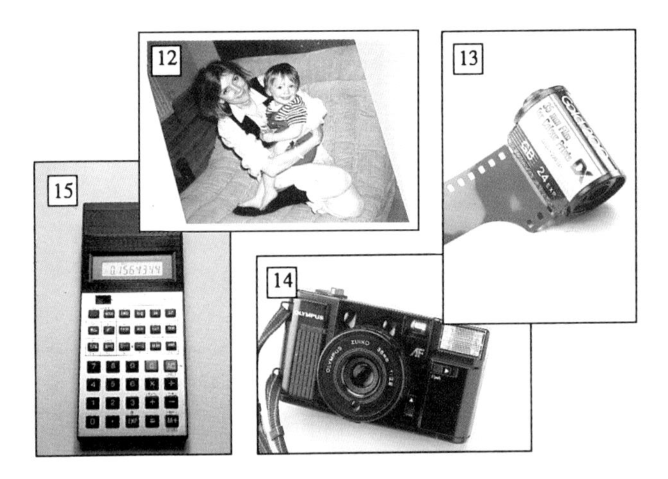

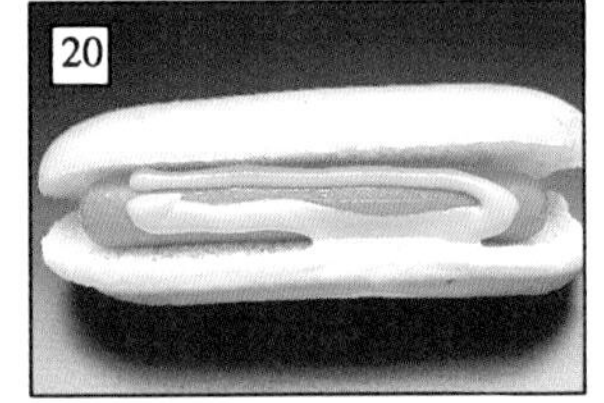

- ☐ taxi
- ☐ jumbo jet
- ☐ police
- ☐ bus
- ☐ satellite
- ☐ helicopter

- ☐ cassette
- ☐ telephone
- ☐ television
- ☐ computer
- ☐ video

- ☐ camera
- ☐ photograph
- ☐ film
- ☐ calculator

- ☐ tennis
- ☐ football

- ☐ hamburger
- ☐ sandwich
- ☐ pizza
- ☐ hot dog

- ☐ restaura
- ☐ superma
- ☐ cinema

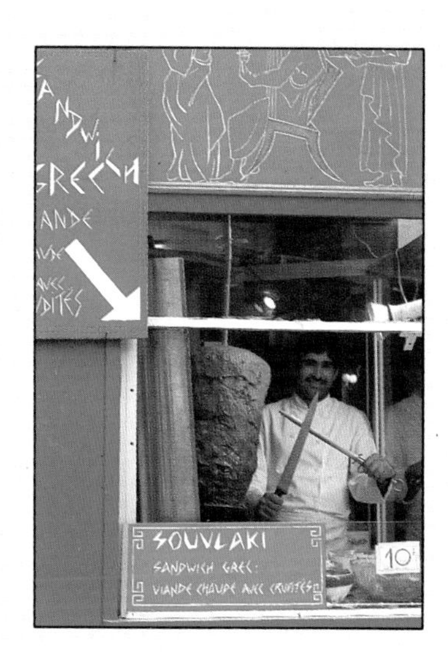

English	My language
video	
telephone	
television	
radio	
computer	
cassette	
camera	
photograph	
film	
sandwich	
buffet	
sport	
pizza	
cafe	
cinema	
taxi	
football	
tennis	
police	
jet	

English word square

Find English words.
8 = good, 10 = very good, 14 = fantastic!

F O O T B A L L G P
H C J E T I Y E S O
J O O L E R M B J L
E M V E P A T A X I
A P W V I D E O B C
N U L I A I N U Y E
S T X S R O N O E K
D E J I T F I L M Z
N R Q O D I S C F C
S S A N D W I C H J

More English words?

Write ten English words.

1 ______ 6 ______
2 ______ 7 ______
3 ______ 8 ______
4 ______ 9 ______
5 ______ 10 ______

10 ten **9** nine **8** eight **7** seven **6** six **5** five **4** four **3** three **2** two **1** one

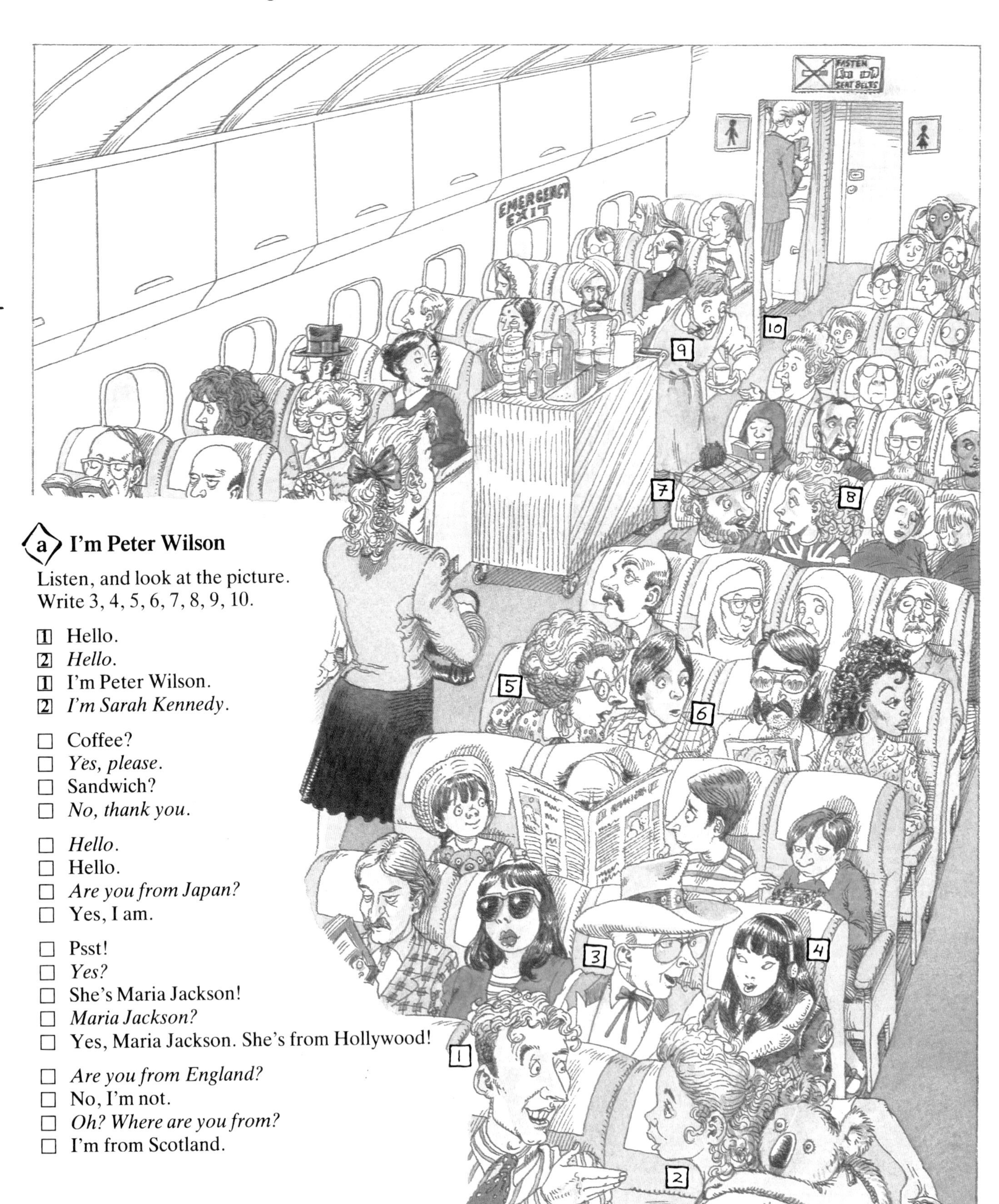

(a) I'm Peter Wilson

Listen, and look at the picture.
Write 3, 4, 5, 6, 7, 8, 9, 10.

[1] Hello.
[2] *Hello.*
[1] I'm Peter Wilson.
[2] *I'm Sarah Kennedy.*

☐ Coffee?
☐ *Yes, please.*
☐ Sandwich?
☐ *No, thank you.*

☐ *Hello.*
☐ Hello.
☐ *Are you from Japan?*
☐ Yes, I am.

☐ Psst!
☐ *Yes?*
☐ She's Maria Jackson!
☐ *Maria Jackson?*
☐ Yes, Maria Jackson. She's from Hollywood!

☐ *Are you from England?*
☐ No, I'm not.
☐ *Oh? Where are you from?*
☐ I'm from Scotland.

b Where's he from?/Where's she from?

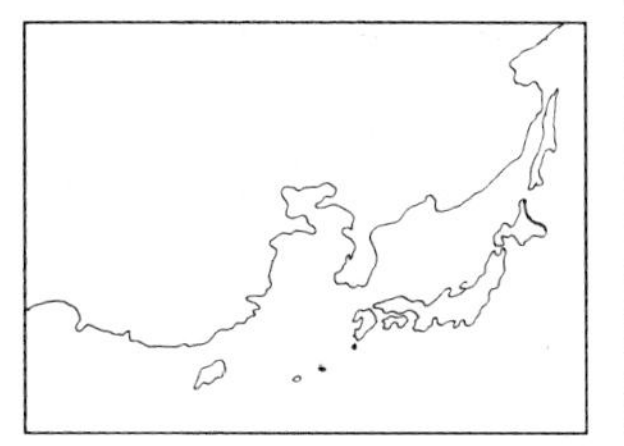
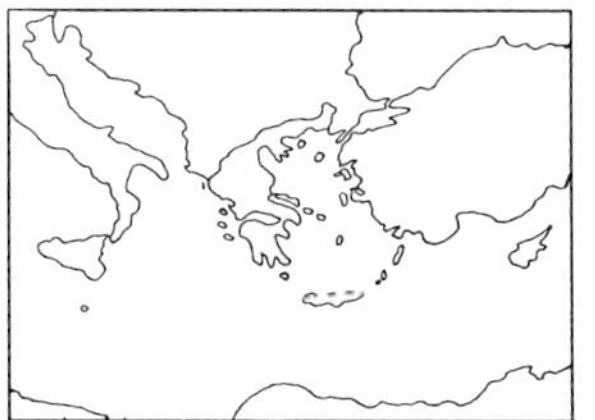
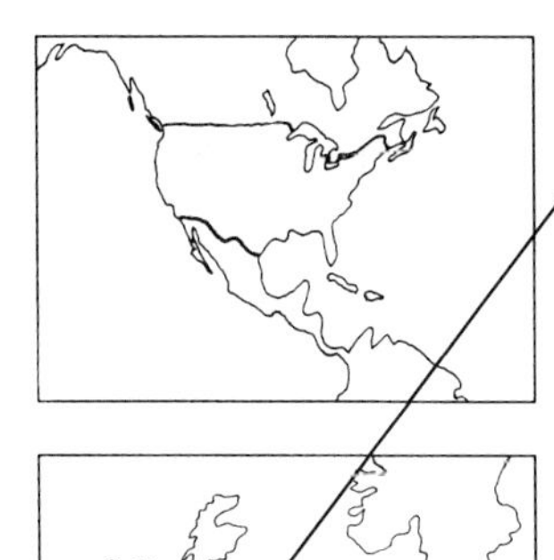

England
Mars
Brazil
Australia
Spain
Japan
The United States
Italy
Greece
France

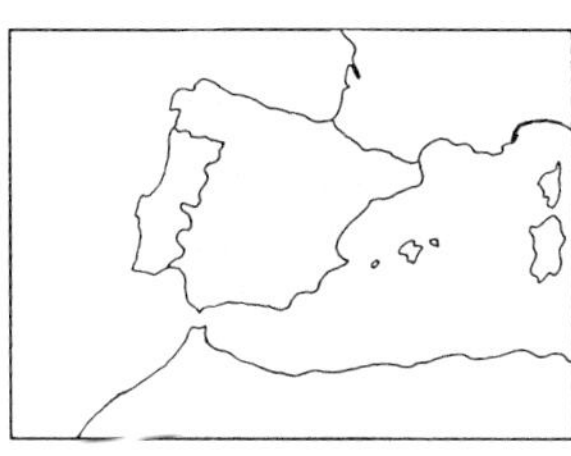

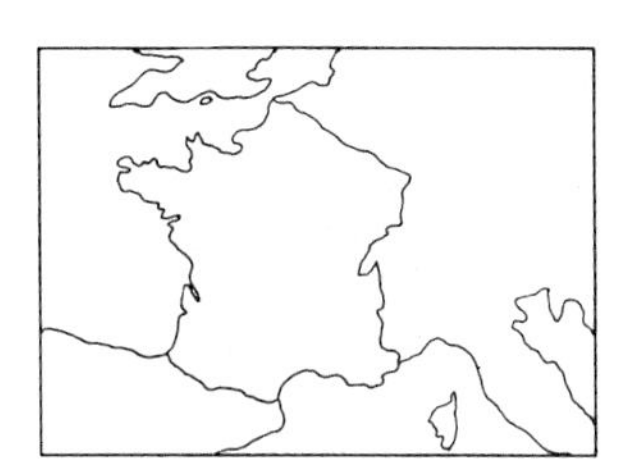

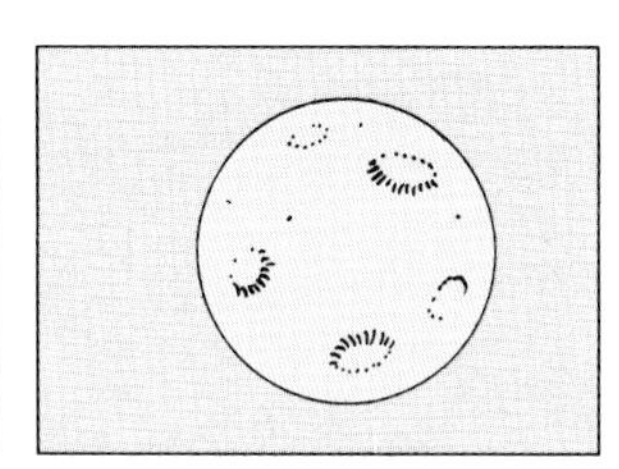

1 Peter Wilson 2 Sarah Kennedy 3 Monique Lefort 4 Yoko Suzuki 5 Maria Jackson

6 João Medeiros 7 Pedro García 8 Paola Bonetti 9 Zog 10 Eleni Dima

c Conversations

Look at the pictures, and make conversations.

1
A *Is he from France?*
B *No, he isn't.*
A *Is he from England?*
B *Yes, he is.*

2
A *She's Paola Bonetti.*
B *Where's she from?*
A *She's from Italy.*

3
A *Are you from England?*
B *No, I'm not.*
A *Where are you from?*
B *I'm from Australia.*

d Hello

Ten, nine, eight, seven, six,
five, four, three, two, one.
Hello, I'm from the stars.
How are you?
Hello, I'm from Mars.
How are you?

Ten, nine, eight, seven, six,
five, four, three, two, one.
Hello, she's from the stars.
How are you?
Hello, she's from Mars.
How are you?

Ten, nine, eight, seven, six,
five, four, three, two, one.
Hello, you're from the Earth.
How are you?
Hello, you're from the Earth.
How are you?

Self-service

a Food

Look at 11 in the picture.
Write 12, 13, 14, 15, 16, 17, 18, 19.

11 eleven: a sandwich
12 twelve: a hot dog
13 thirteen: a hamburger
14 fourteen: a salad
15 fifteen: an apple pie
16 sixteen: an orange juice
17 seventeen: an ice cream
18 eighteen: a tea
19 nineteen: a coffee

SANDWICH BAR

cheese sandwich	60p
tuna sandwich	90p
chicken sandwich	80p
tea	40p
coffee	50p
cola	70p

11 Good morning.
12 Good morning.
11 A cheese sandwich, please.
12 OK. Anything else?
11 Yes. A tea, please.
12 Here you are.
11 Thanks.

SALAD CENTRE

egg salad	£ 2.20
cheese salad	£ 2.10
chicken salad	£ 2.30
tuna salad	£ 2.40
egg sandwich	90p
apple juice / orange juice	70p
Pepsi-Cola / 7-Up	40p
ice cream	70p
apple pie	80p

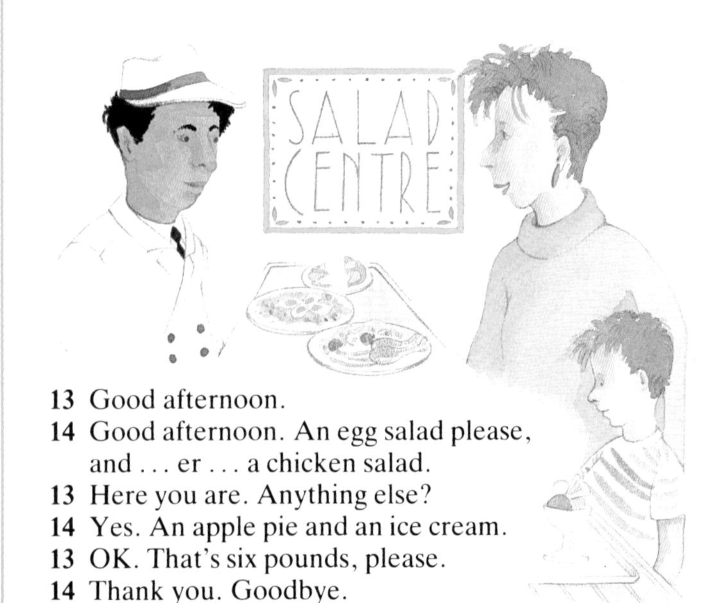

13 Good afternoon.
14 Good afternoon. An egg salad please, and . . . er . . . a chicken salad.
13 Here you are. Anything else?
14 Yes. An apple pie and an ice cream.
13 OK. That's six pounds, please.
14 Thank you. Goodbye.
13 Goodbye.

20 twenty **30** thirty **40** forty **50** fifty **60** sixty **70** seventy **80** eighty **90** ninety

HAMBURGER HOUSE	
hamburger	£ 1.50
cheeseburger	£ 2.00
pizza	£ 1.30
ice cream	£ 1.20
orange juice / apple juice	50p
tea / coffee	50p

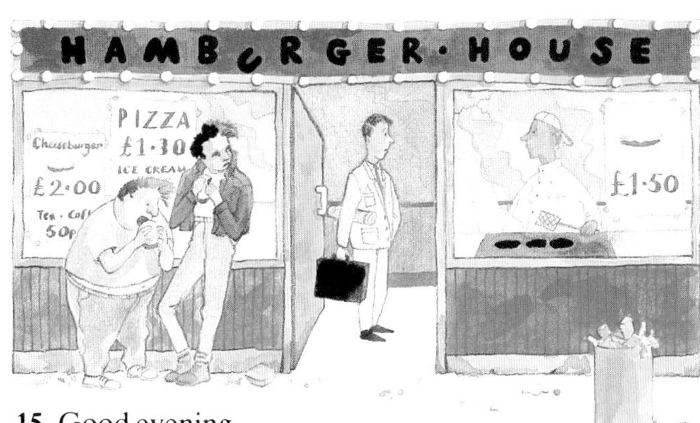

15 Good evening.
16 Good evening. A hamburger, please.
15 Pardon?
16 A hamburger, please. And an orange juice.
15 A hamburger and an orange juice?
16 Yes, please.
15 That's two pounds.
16 Two pounds . . . here you are. Thank you.
15 Thank you. Good night.
16 Good night.

17 John!
18 Daniel! Hello, how are you?
17 I'm very well, thanks. And you?
18 I'm fine.
17 And Stephen . . . how's Stephen?
18 Oh, he's fine . . .

a	**an** (a e i o u)
a hamburger	an apple juice
a cheese sandwich	an egg salad
a tuna salad	an ice cream
a coffee	an orange juice

b  Four conversations

Listen to the four conversations.
Put ticks [✓] in the boxes.

	1	2	3	4
Salad				
egg	✓			
cheese				
chicken				
tuna				
Sandwich				
egg				
cheese				
chicken				
tuna				
Drink				
orange juice	✓			
apple juice				
tea				
Dessert				
ice cream				
apple pie	✓			

Is it a star?

Anne Look!
Laura Where?
Anne Over there. What is it?
Laura I don't know. Is it an aeroplane?
Anne No, it isn't an aeroplane.
Laura Is it a star?
Anne No, it isn't. What is it, Laura?
Laura I don't know, Anne . . . I don't know . . .

Mike Is it open?
Ken Yeah. It's open. Look!
Mike What are they?
Ken I don't know. Are they televisions?
Mike No, they aren't televisions.
Ken Are they computers?
Mike No, they aren't. They're videos!
Ken Listen! What's that?
Mike Oh no! It's a police car!

a What is it?/What are they?

radio, cassette player, television, video, speaker, computer
1 *It's a television. / They're televisions.*
Write five more sentences.

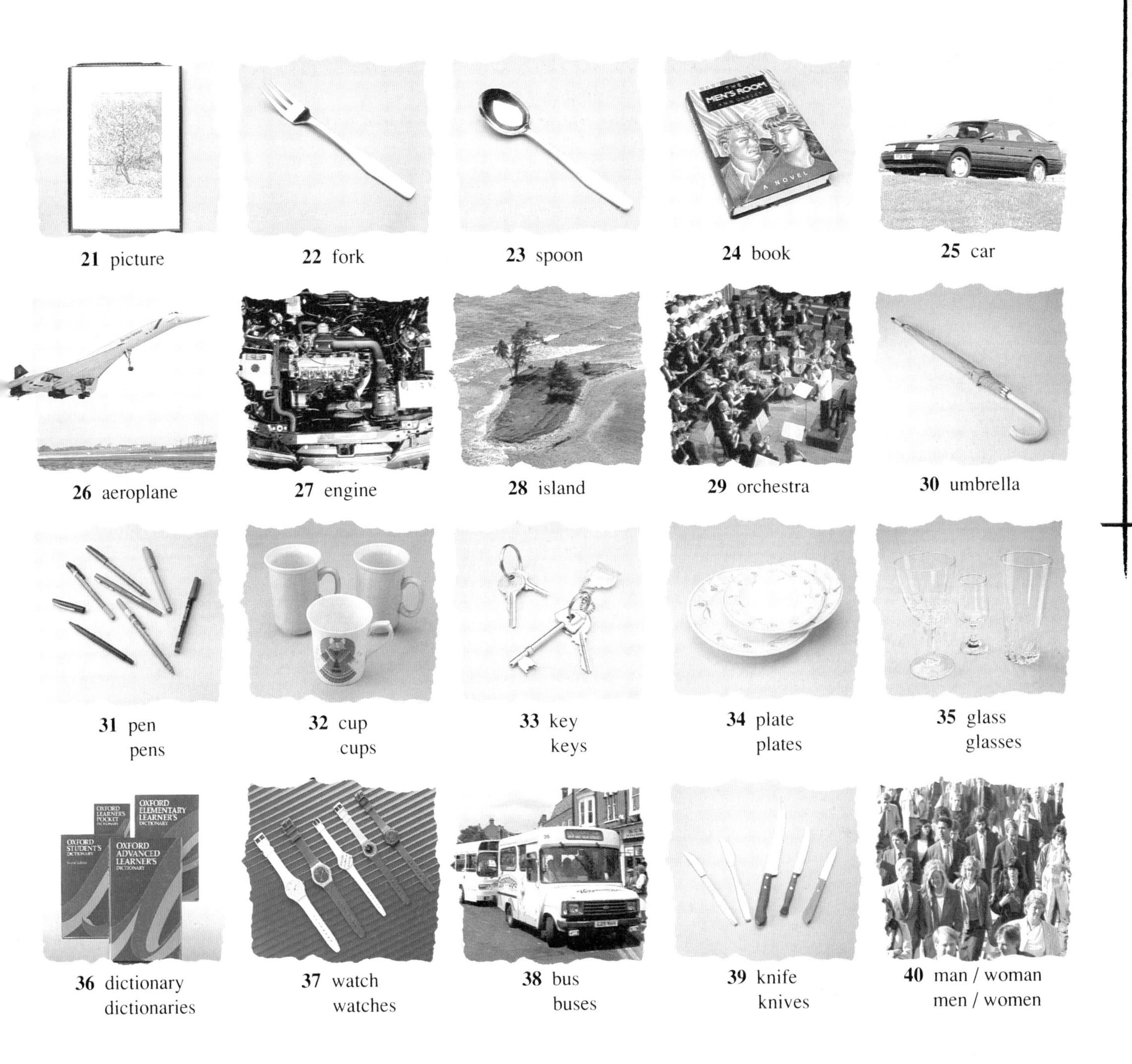

21 picture
22 fork
23 spoon
24 book
25 car
26 aeroplane
27 engine
28 island
29 orchestra
30 umbrella
31 pen / pens
32 cup / cups
33 key / keys
34 plate / plates
35 glass / glasses
36 dictionary / dictionaries
37 watch / watches
38 bus / buses
39 knife / knives
40 man / woman / men / women

b Game

Look at the pictures for two minutes.
Student A: Open the book.
Student B: Close the book.

A *What's number 22?*
B *It's a fork. / I don't know.*
A *What's number 36?*
B *They're dictionaries. / I don't know.*

c Bingo!

Write nine numbers (between 21 and 99) in Box 1, and nine numbers in Box 2.

Box 1

Box 2

Names and addresses

- ■ What's his name?
- □ I don't know. What's his number?
- ■ Er . . . he's number seven.
- □ Oh! His name's Gary Taylor.
- ■ Gary Taylor? Where's he from?
- □ He's from Liverpool. He's fantastic! Look!

a What's your name?

Listen to the conversations. Match A E, I O, U Y to the picture.

A Come here, Smith!
E My name isn't Smith . . .
A What *is* your name?
E Taylor. I'm Gary Taylor.
A Oh. What's your number?
E I'm number seven. Smith is number two.
A Oh, sorry.
E That's OK.
A It isn't OK . . . to the dressing room!
E What?
A Go to the dressing room, Taylor! Go now!

I I'm lost!
O Oh dear. What's your name?
I Kevin . . .
O What's your surname, Kevin?
I Stewart.
O And what's your address?
I Um . . . 132 Waterloo Street, Tottenham, London.
O What's your telephone number?
I Um . . . 081–656–4893.

U Name?
Y What?
U What's your name?
Y Paine.
U Paine? Spell it.
Y P-A-I-N-E.
U First name?
Y Darren.
U Address?
Y 207 Redhill Road, Bristol.
U Phone number?
Y Bristol 901332.
U OK, Paine. Come this way . . .

b Numbers

100 – one hundred
200 – two hundred
305 – three hundred and five

Number: **188**
Say *one hundred and eighty-eight.*

Telephone number: **21880**
Say *two – one – double eight – oh.*

1 Say these numbers:
100 104 212 327 439
561 655 792 848 910

2 Say these telephone numbers:
33210 55677 48990 311664

c The alphabet

1 Say:

A H J K
B C D E G P T V
F L M N S X
I Y
U W
O Q R Z

2 Say:
USA ITV EEC VW
BBC UFO OK MG

d Programmes

Look at number 8 on the football programme.

A *What's his first name?*
B *Gary.*

A *What's his surname? Spell it.*
B *Jones. J-O-N-E-S.*

A *Where's he from?*
B *He's from Liverpool.*

Ask and answer about the other players on the programmes.

e Chart

	1	2	You	Your partner
Surname	Brown	Talbot		
First name(s)	Rachel Maria	Gary David		
Address	350 Bridge Street Liverpool	17 North Road Southampton		
Telephone number	051-677-3288	0703-22991		

What's her surname? / What's her first name? / What are her first names?
What's her address? / What's her telephone number?

1 Ask and answer about numbers 1 and 2.
2 Write in your name, address, and telephone number.
3 Talk to your partner. Write in his/her name, address, and telephone number.

f Three people

Surname ______ ______ ______
First name(s) ______ ______ ______
Address ______ ______ ______
Telephone number ______ ______ ______

1 Listen to the three people.
Write in the names, addresses, and telephone numbers.

2 Ask and answer about the people.

INTERNATIONAL FOOTBALL ENGLAND v SCOTLAND

WEMBLEY STADIUM 14 MAY 3.00pm

ENGLAND

Goalkeeper

1
Roy Clement
(Southampton)

Defenders

2
Gary Smith
(Tottenham)

3
Brian Roberts
(Manchester United)

4
Daniel McQueen
(Everton)

5
Kevin Fox
(Birmingham)

Midfield players

6
Trevor Page
(Tottenham)

7
Gary Taylor
(Liverpool)

8
Gary Jones
(Liverpool)

Strikers

9
Kevin Stevens
(Everton)

10
Steve Wade
(Manchester United)

11
Darren Fitzroy
(Newcastle)

Women's Tennis Championship semi-finals

Wimbledon 29 June 2.00pm

Rachel Patworth *(Great Britain)*
v
Martina Kundera *(Czechoslovakia)*

Doris Decker *(United States of America)*
v
Caroline Dundee *(Australia)*

Lambert and Stacey

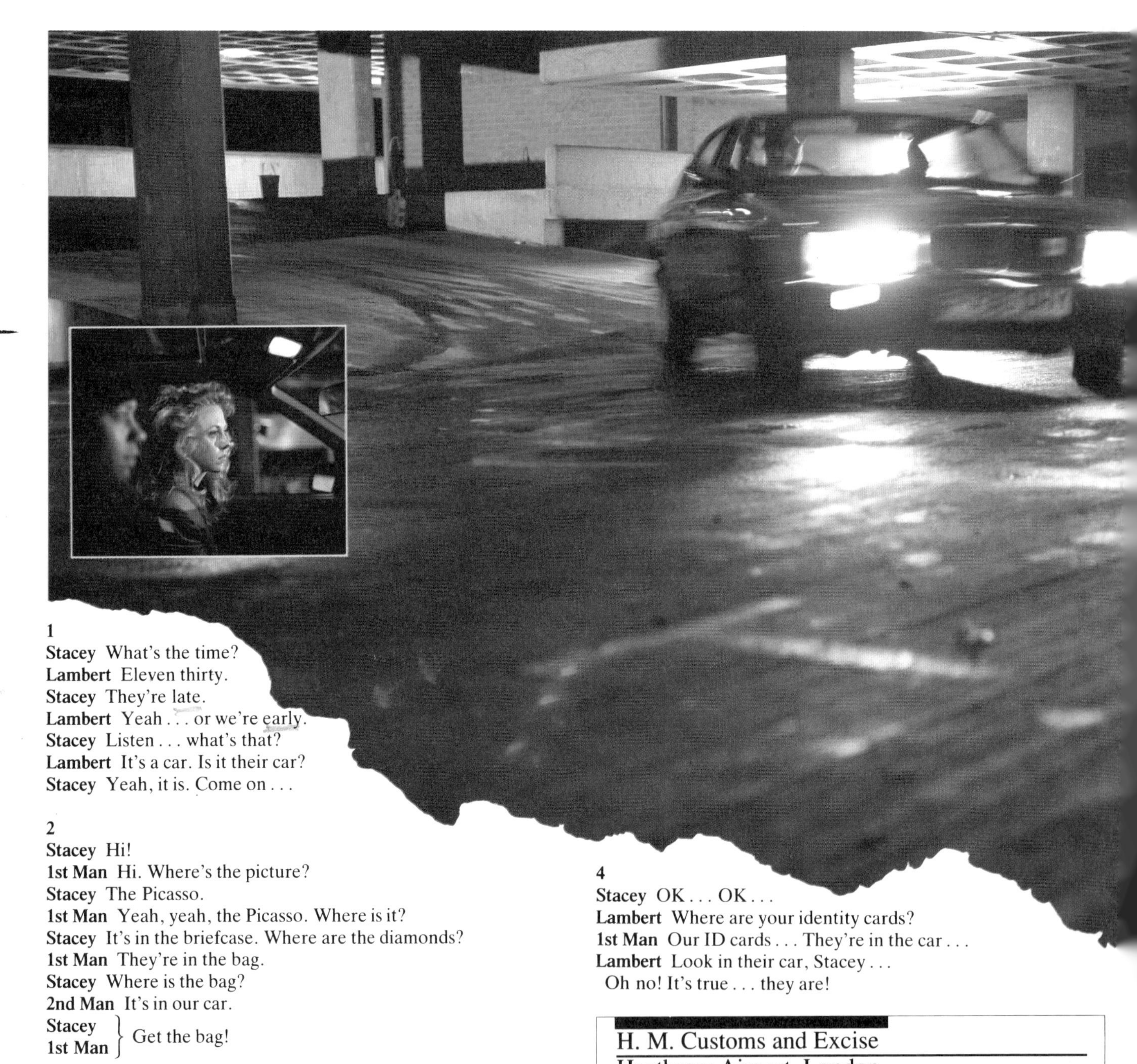

1
Stacey What's the time?
Lambert Eleven thirty.
Stacey They're late.
Lambert Yeah . . . or we're early.
Stacey Listen . . . what's that?
Lambert It's a car. Is it their car?
Stacey Yeah, it is. Come on . . .

2
Stacey Hi!
1st Man Hi. Where's the picture?
Stacey The Picasso.
1st Man Yeah, yeah, the Picasso. Where is it?
Stacey It's in the briefcase. Where are the diamonds?
1st Man They're in the bag.
Stacey Where is the bag?
2nd Man It's in our car.
Stacey / **1st Man** } Get the bag!

3
1st Man Right . . . here you are.
Stacey Thanks.
Lambert OK, hands on the car! I'm Lambert, she's Stacey. We're detectives . . .
1st Man You're detectives . . .
Stacey Police.
2nd Man They *are* detectives.
1st Man But *we* aren't criminals . . .
Stacey Huh!
1st Man We're customs officers . . . from the airport.
2nd Man We're detectives, too.

4
Stacey OK . . . OK . . .
Lambert Where are your identity cards?
1st Man Our ID cards . . . They're in the car . . .
Lambert Look in their car, Stacey . . . Oh no! It's true . . . they are!

H. M. Customs and Excise
Heathrow Airport, London

Surname: Ross
First name(s): David Charles
Title: Inspector of Customs
Number: W342-6771

a What's the time?

A *What's the time?*
B *It's six o'clock.*

A *What's the time?*
B *It's ten forty.*

A *What's the time?*
B *It's eleven thirty.*

Continue:

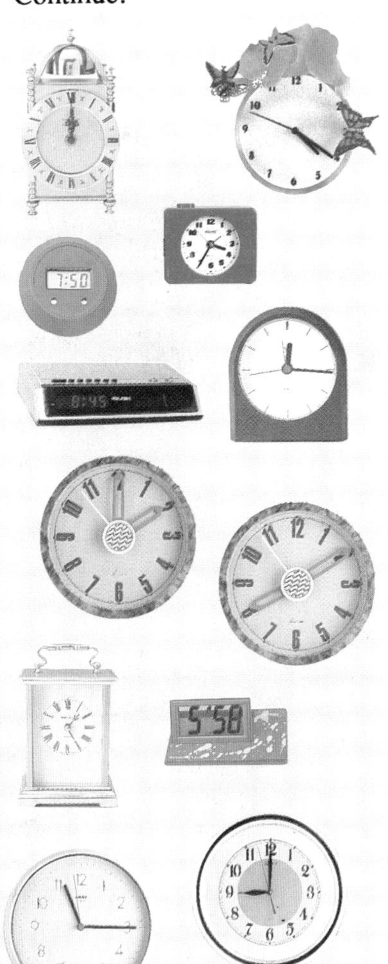

Dear Sarah and Ben,
Hi! This is a picture of our plane It's an Airbus. We're in London! Do you know Gary and Eva Ford? Well, they're in London too. They're in our hotel. Our room is number 321, and their room is number 322! Our suitcases aren't in London. But they aren't lost... they're in Manchester. Gary and Eva aren't happy. Their suitcases are in Tokyo!
Best Wishes
Karen and David

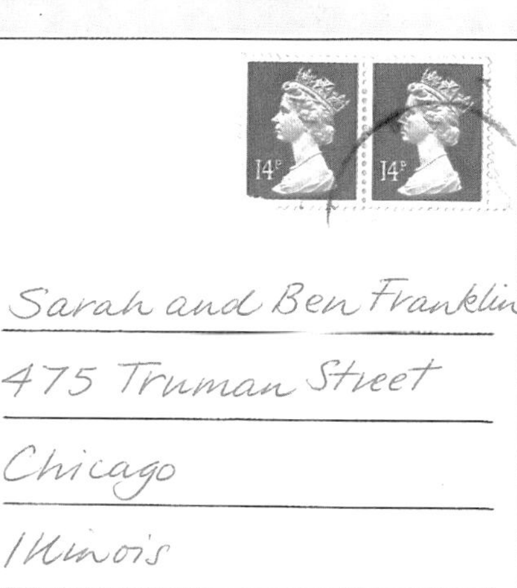

Sarah and Ben Franklin
475 Truman Street
Chicago
Illinois
60615 U.S.A.

b Questions

Ask and answer.

1. Is their plane a Boeing 767?
2. What is it?
3. Are Karen and David in Chicago?
4. Where are they?
5. Are their suitcases in London?
6. Are their suitcases lost?
7. Where are their suitcases?
8. Where are Gary and Eva?
9. What is their room number?
10. Where are their suitcases?
11. Where are Sarah and Ben?
12. What is their address?

c Registration

Look at the registration card.
Complete the conversation.

Karen Good afternoon.
Receptionist ______ , ______ names?
Karen Our ______ Karen and David Kennedy.
Receptionist ______ students?
Karen No, ______ . We ______ .
Receptionist Where ______ from?
Karen ______ .
Receptionist ______ passport numbers?
Karen ______ and ______ .
Receptionist ______ address?
Karen ______ .
Receptionist OK, you're in room ______ . Where are your suitcases?
Karen Ah! ______ !

HOLIDAY HOTEL
4-8 Stone Street
London SW1 8NT
Tel: (01) 567 1245

Guest Registration Card

Family name KENNEDY
First name(s) KAREN & DAVID
Occupation TEACHERS
Nationality AMERICAN
Passport number(s) 2442890/W318500
Home address 471 TRUMAN ST. CHICAGO, ILLINOIS, 60615, USA
Room number 321

d Role play

Student A is the receptionist at the hotel. Student B is a guest.
Look at the guest registration card.
Have a conversation.

The London train

Driver This is the station.
Philip Thank you. How much is that?
Driver Three pounds fifty.
Philip And where's the ticket office?
Driver It's over there. That's the ticket office. It's next to the entrance.

Diana Good afternoon.
Girl 'Afternoon.
Diana Two tickets to London, please.
Girl Single or return?
Diana Return, please. How much?
Girl Twenty-four pounds.
Diana Here you are.
Girl Thanks.
Diana What time's the next train?
Girl Seventeen forty.

Philip Excuse m
Guard Yes?
Philip Is this the Lonc train?
Guard No, it isn't. That's t' London train over ther
Philip Where?
Guard On platform three.
Philip Thank you.

Diana Excuse me . . .
Man Yes?
Diana Are these seats free?
Man No, sorry. They aren't. But *those* seats are free.
Diana Where?
Man Over there. Next to the door.
Diana Thank you.

Diana Philip! Those aren't my bags!
Philip Aren't they?
Diana No. *These* are my bags!
Philip OK. Well, we're here. This is London.

a Where's the ticket office?

Look at the railway station.

A *Where's the ticket office?*
B *It's next to the exit.*
A *Where are the toilets?*
B *They're next to the news kiosk.*

Ask and answer about the station.

b How much?

A *How much is that?*
How much is it?
How much?

B *It's three pounds fifty.*

Ask and answer about the tickets.

c Departures

information Departures [17.32]

TIME	DESTINATION	PLATFORM
17.30	Portsmouth	4
17.35	Oxford, Birmingham, Liverpool	1
17.40	London	3
17.50	Bournemouth, Poole	4
18.10	Winchester	1
18.20	Manchester	3
18.50	Bournemouth, Weymouth	4
19.00	London	3

Note: 16.00 – Say *sixteen hundred* (or *four o'clock*).

A *What time's the Portsmouth train?*
B *Seventeen thirty.*

Ask and answer about the departures board.

d Announcements

Listen. Write the times and platform numbers.

Time	Destination	Platform
1 *20.40*	London	*4*
2	Oxford	....
3	Bournemouth	....
4	Manchester, Liverpool	....
5	Portsmouth	....

Space station

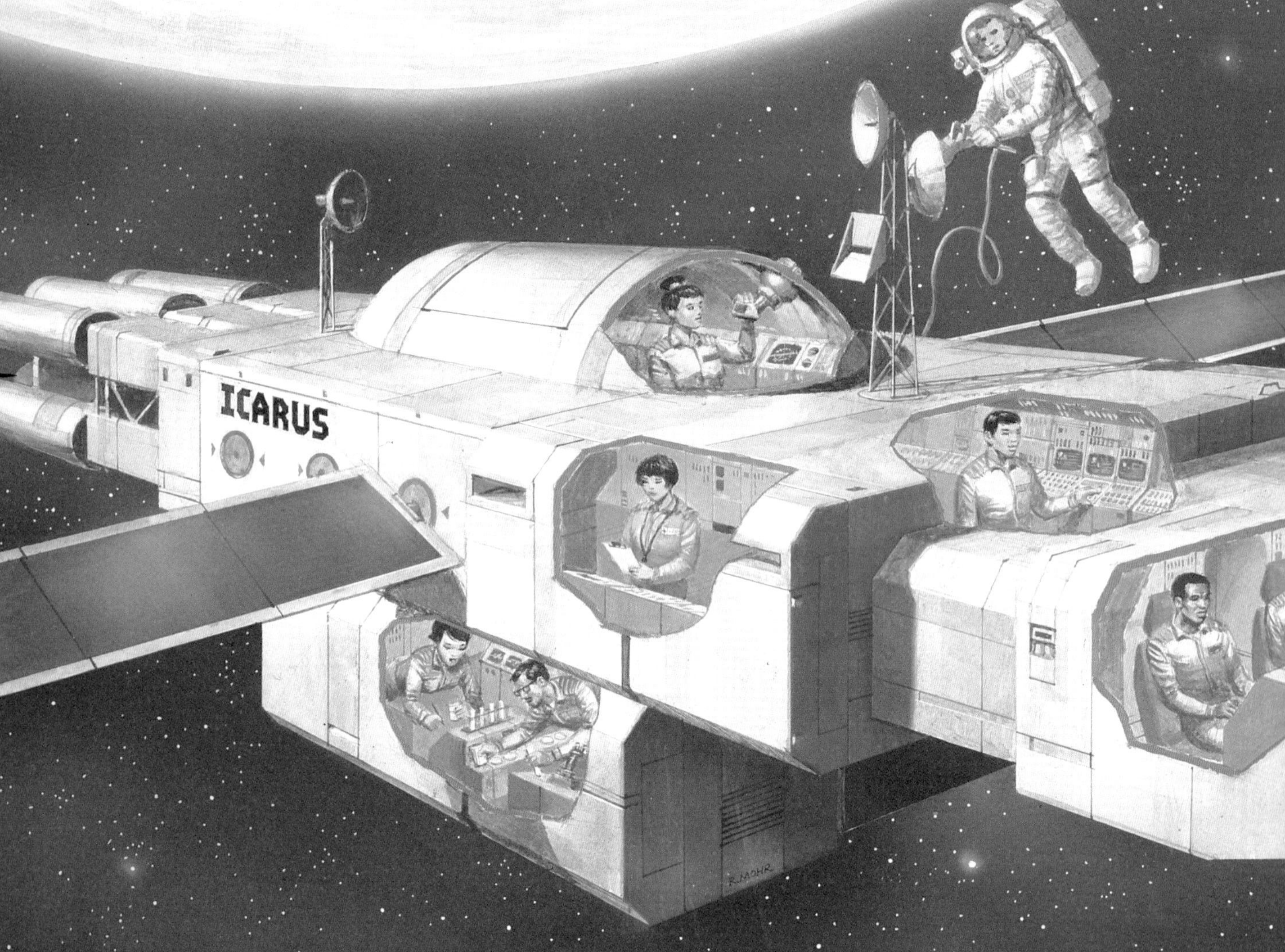

This is the crew of the new space station, 'Icarus'. They are from eight countries. Icarus is an international space station, and it is nine thousand kilometres above the Earth.

CLARKE ASIMOV

Peter Clarke and Ivan Asimov are the pilots. Peter's American, and Ivan's Russian. Peter's thirty-two, and he's from Los Angeles. Ivan is forty, and he's from Moscow.

 VERNE

Marie Verne is twenty-nine, and she's the doctor on Icarus. Marie is French. She's from Paris.

 BALLARD

Mark Ballard is British, and he's the engineer. Mark is thirty-two, and he's from London.

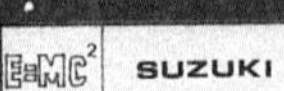 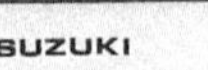 
SUZUKI MARQUEZ

Yoko Suzuki and Antonio Marquez are the scientists on the space station. She's thirty-one, and she's from Tokyo. She's Japanese. He's thirty-two, and he's Spanish. He's from Madrid.

 LI

Li Song is Chinese. He's the computer specialist. He's twenty-eight years old, and he's from Shanghai.

 CABRAL

Cristina Cabral is Brazilian. She's from Rio de Janeiro, and she's the astronomer on Icarus. She's twenty-nine years old.

1957 Laika, a dog, first traveller in space ... 1961 Yuri Gagarin, first man in space ... 1963 Valentina Tereshkova, first

a Crew chart

Complete the chart.

Name	Age	Nationality	Home town	Job
Peter Clarke				
Ivan Asimov				
Marie Verne				
Mark Ballard				
Yoko Suzuki				
Antonio Marquez				
Li Song				
Cristina Cabral				

b Questions

Ask and answer.

1. Who are the pilots?
2. Who is the astronomer?
3. Who is from Japan?
4. Who is from Paris?
5. Who are the scientists?
6. Who is Spanish?
7. Who is forty years old?
8. Who is the computer specialist?
9. Who is from Rio de Janeiro?
10. Who is thirty-one?

c Who is she?

A *Who is she?*
B *She's Marie Verne. / She's the doctor.*

A *Who are they?*
B *They're Yoko and Antonio. / They're the scientists.*

Make questions and answers about the crew.

d How old is he?

A *How old is Li Song?*
B *He's twenty-eight. / He's twenty-eight years old.*

A *How old are Marie and Cristina?*
B *They're twenty-nine. / They're twenty-nine years old.*

Make questions and answers about the crew.

e What's his job?

A *What's his job?*
B *He's an engineer. / He's the engineer on Icarus.*

A *What are their jobs?*
B *They're pilots. / They're the pilots on Icarus.*

Make questions and answers about the crew.

What's her nationality?

1 Complete the chart with these words:
Spanish French Japanese Russian
Brazilian British Chinese.

The United States American	The USSR ________
Britain ________	Spain ________
China ________	Japan ________
Brazil ________	France ________

2 Look at the chart.

A *Marie's from France. What's her nationality?*
B *She's French.*
A *Where's she from?*
B *She's from Paris.*

Make questions and answers about the crew.

Thousands

6,000 – six thousand
3,451 – three thousand four hundred and fifty-one
Say these numbers:

2,987	**1,207**	**4,361**	**9,400**	**2,000**
5,100	**9,001**	**3,820**	**10,000**	**8,510**

Interviews

You are a reporter. Interview the crew. Ask about:
name, age, nationality, home town, job.

Game: Who is it?

Student A: Close your book.
Student B: Look at the space station.
Think of one of the crew.
Student A: Ask questions, and find the crew member.

Who are you?

Ask another student questions. Write his/her:
name, age, nationality, home town, job.

... 1969 Neil Armstrong, first man on the moon... 1973 Skylab space station ...1975 American astronauts and Russian

What's it like?

Is this your new car?

It's the fantastic first prize in our new competition!!!
Win a Jaguar XJ6!
The XJ6 3.6 is £28,000!

Second Prize

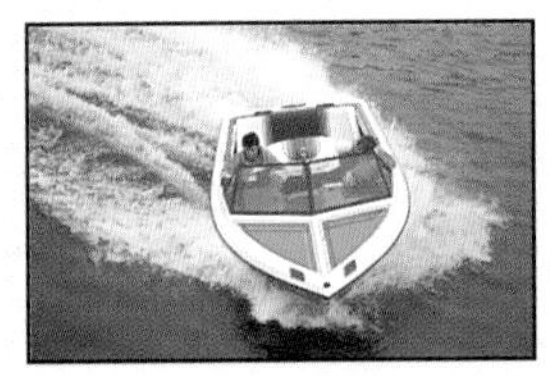

Malibu Skier sports boat - 70 kph
American - £14,750

Third Prize

Four Samsonite *Oyster* suitcases
British - £320 for the four

Fourth Prize

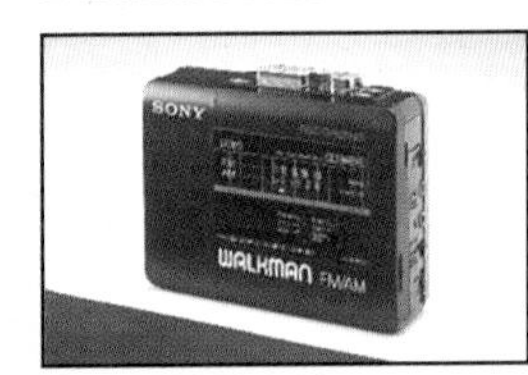

Sony Walkman personal stereo
Model WM - F66
Japanese - £65

Number the words below from 1 to 6.

☐ fast ☐ British ☐ new
☐ big ☐ beautiful ☐ expensive

Write your name and address on the form, and send it to:

JAGUAR Competition
The Weekend Magazine
P.O. Box 54
London, E2 8RJ

Name: ______________
Address: ______________
____
____

Kate Paul! Look at this letter! I'm the winner of the competition!
Paul What competition?
Kate The competition in *The Weekend Magazine*. I'm the winner . . .
Paul What's the prize?
Kate It's a new car.
Paul A new car? What make is it?
Kate It's a Jaguar.
Paul Fantastic! What's it like?
Kate It's beautiful. It's big, and fast . . .
Paul . . . and it's our car!
Kate Well . . . my car . . .
Paul What colour is it?
Kate I don't know . . .
Paul Look at the letter.
Kate Ergh! It's pink!

a Role play

Make conversations about the 2nd prize, the 3rd prize, and the 4th pri
Note
What's the prize?
What are they like?
What colour are they?

white	pink	red	orange	yellow	green	blue	brown	black

1st a calculator
grey
Casio
(Japanese)

2nd jeans
blue
Levis
(American)

3rd a shirt
yellow
Lacoste
(French)

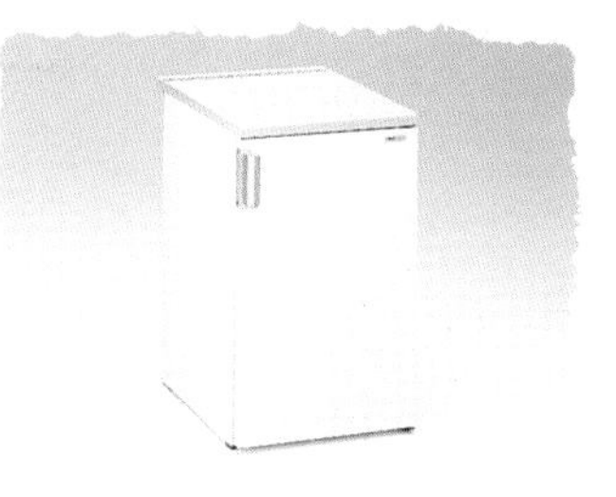

4th a fridge
white
Zanussi
(Italian)

5th a car
red
SEAT
(Spanish)

6th a truck
green
Volvo
(Swedish)

7th a hair dryer
black
Philips
(Dutch)

8th a cooker
brown
Neff
(German)

b What make is it?

Look at the first picture.

A *What's the first picture?*
B *It's a calculator.*
A *What colour is it?*
B *It's grey.*
A *What make is it?*
B *It's a Casio.*
A *Is it English?*
B *No. It isn't. It's Japanese.*

Ask and answer about the pictures.

c Describe them

A *My watch is new. It's a Rolex and it's beautiful. It's an expensive watch.*
B *My jeans are old. They're blue, and they're Wranglers. They aren't expensive jeans.*

Talk about other things, with these words:
new / old big / small expensive / not expensive
fast / slow beautiful / not beautiful

d Flags

A *What colour is the Dutch flag?*
B *It's red, white, and blue.*

Ask and answer about the other flags.

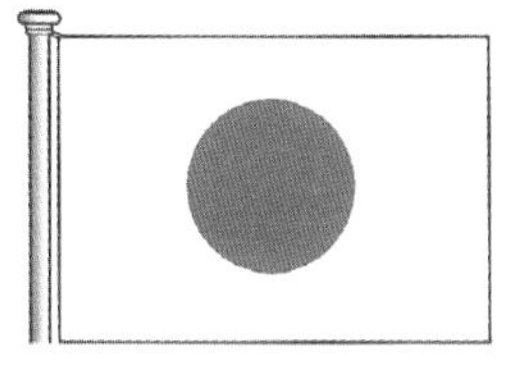

Japan

Sweden

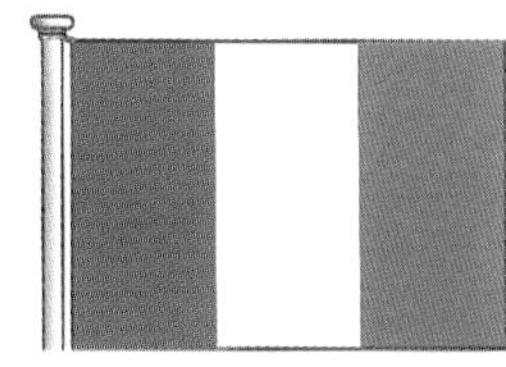

Italy

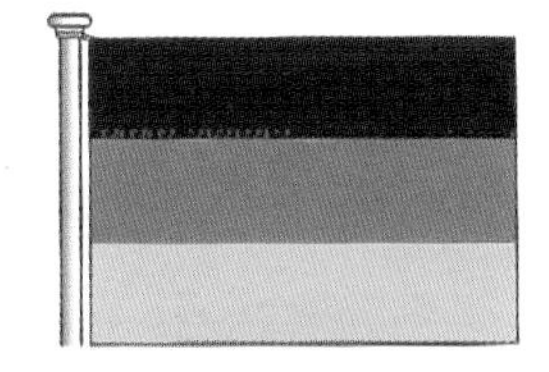

Germany

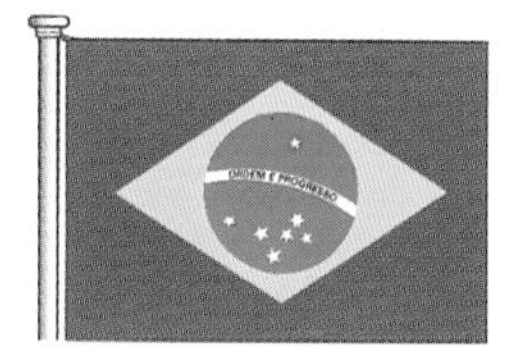

Brazil

Holland

USA

Turkey

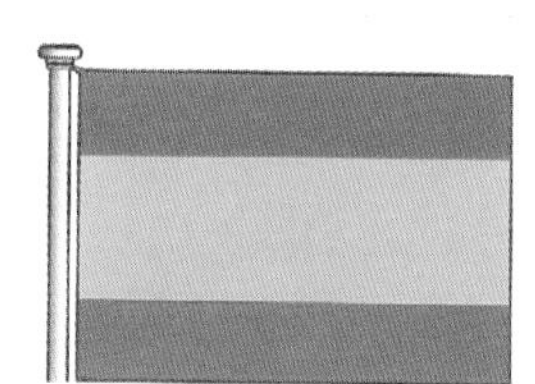

Spain

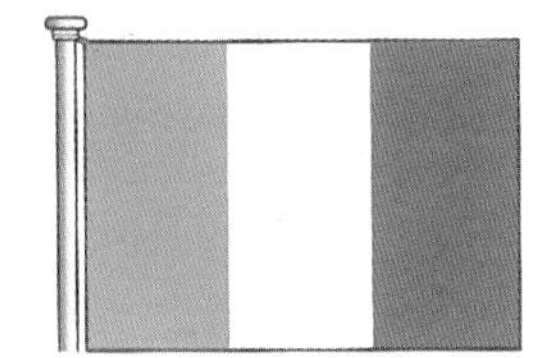

France

Where is she?

WHERE IS SHE?
SHE'S DOWN THERE! SHE'S ON THAT ROCK.

SHE'S BELOW US NOW.

IT'S OK. I'M ABOVE HER.

OH NO! SHE'S IN THE SEA!

SHE'S UNDER THE WATER.
PUT ME DOWN!

IT'S OK, PULL THEM UP.

RIGHT. THEY'RE IN THE HELICOPTER.

MY DOG! HE'S DOWN THERE ON THE ROCK. PLEASE, PLEASE RESCUE HIM.

ERR... IS IT FRIENDLY?

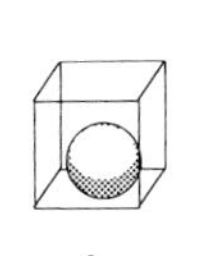
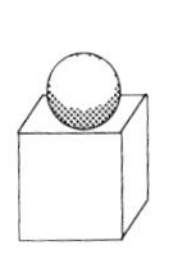
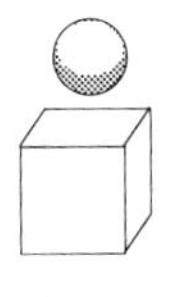
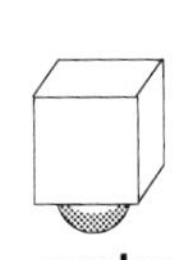

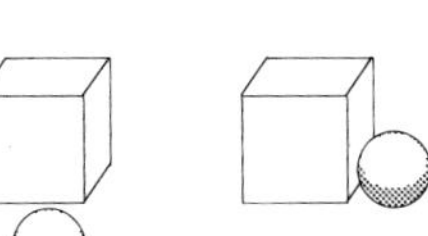
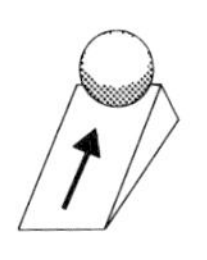
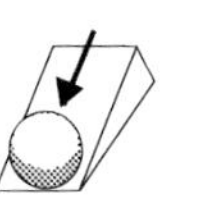
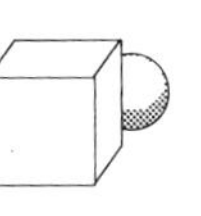
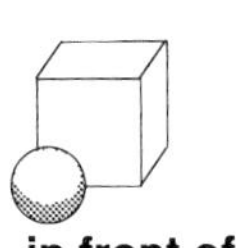

in **on** **above** **under** **below** **next to** **up** **down** **behind** **in front of**

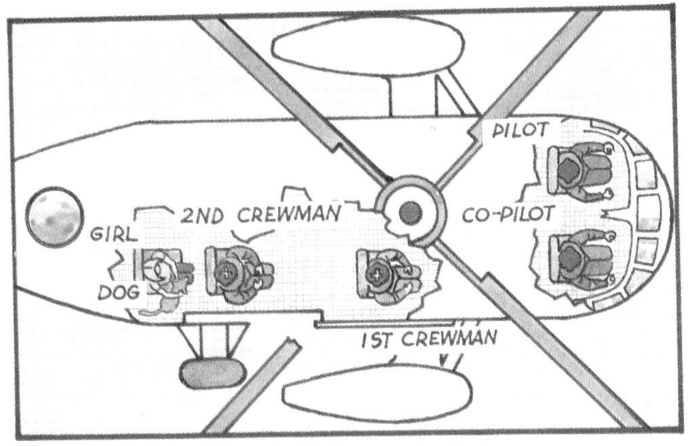

a Where are they?

A *Where's the second crewman?*
B *He's behind the first crewman.*
He's in front of the girl.
He's next to the door.

A *Who's behind the co-pilot?*
B *The first crewman is behind the co-pilot.*

Ask and answer about the people in the helicopter, with *Where?* and *Who?*

b Your class

1 Look at this class plan. Look at Maria.
Who is behind her?
Who is next to her?
Who is in front of her?

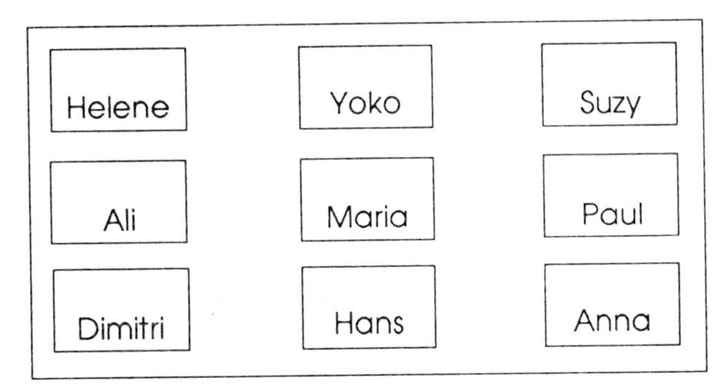

2 Now look at your class.
Who is behind you?
Who is next to you?
Who is in front of you?
Draw a plan of your class.

3 Ask and answer about the plan.

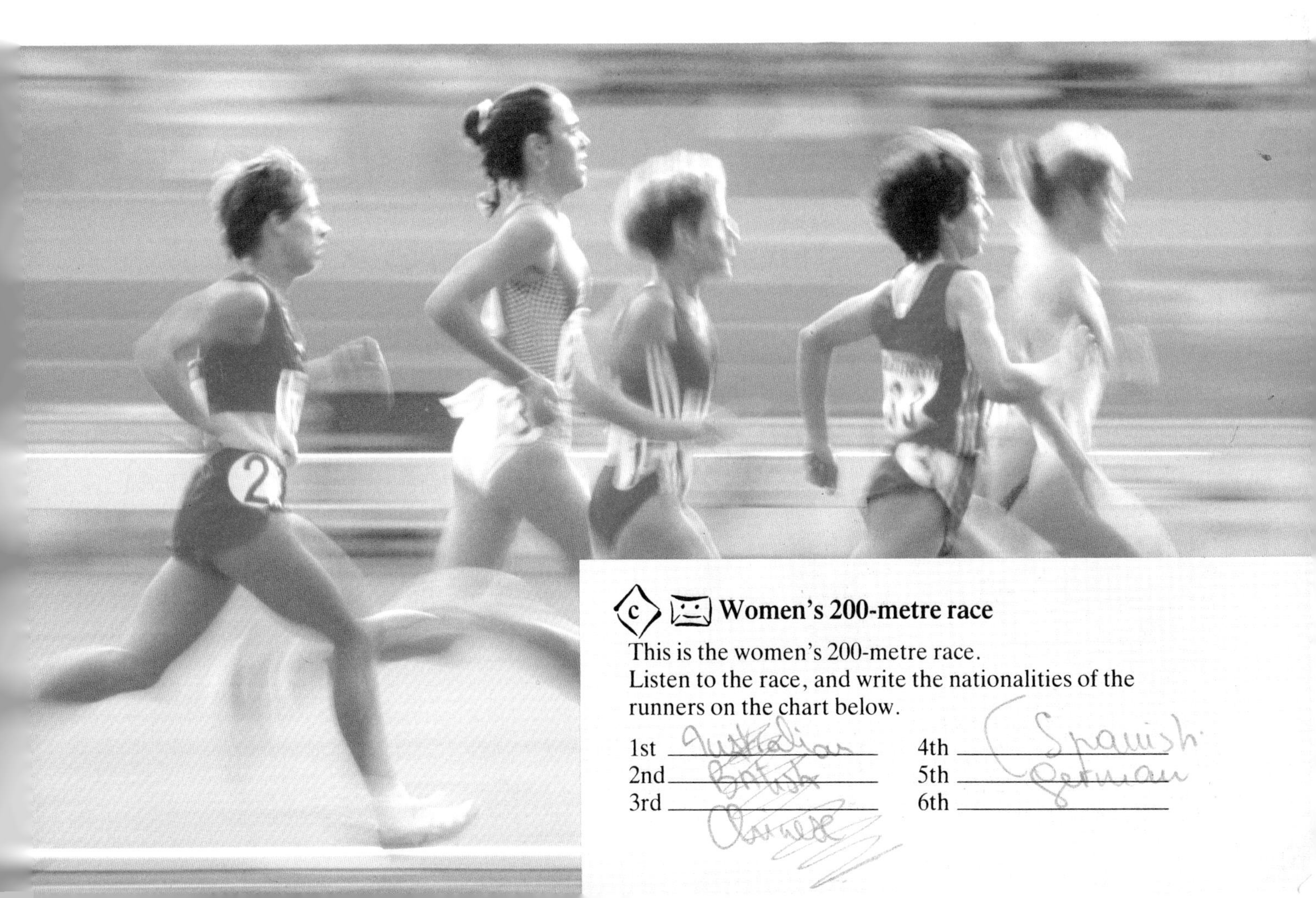

c Women's 200-metre race

This is the women's 200-metre race.
Listen to the race, and write the nationalities of the runners on the chart below.

1st ____________ 4th ____________
2nd ____________ 5th ____________
3rd ____________ 6th ____________

Quiz of the Week

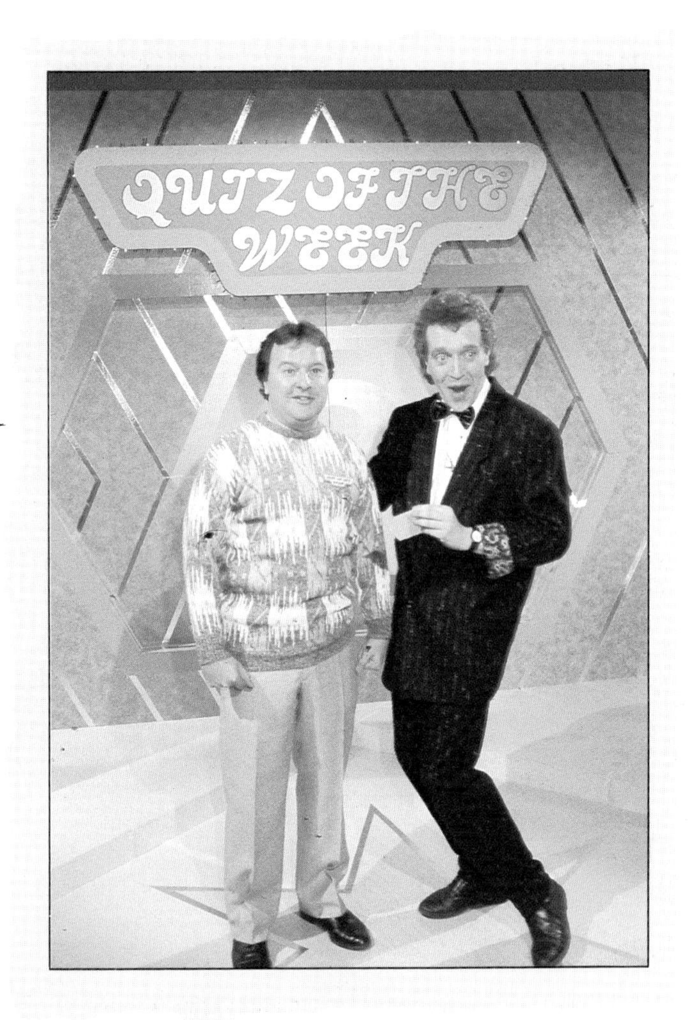

Lesley Good evening, ladies and gentlemen! I'm Lesley Crawley, and welcome to 'Quiz of the Week'. There are some wonderful prizes tonight, and here's our first contestant. It's Mr Frank Miller from London!
Lesley Hello, Frank!
Frank Good evening, Lesley.
Lesley And how are you tonight?
Frank Fine.
Lesley Good. You're in front of me, Frank. Stand next to me . . . no, next to me, that's right.
Frank Sorry.
Lesley Right, here is the first question. What is the capital of France?
Frank Er . . . um . . . I don't know . . . er . . .
Lesley I love *Paris* in the springtime, I love *Paris* in the fall . . .
Frank Is it Paris?
Lesley Yes, that's right, Frank! And now the second question! Where is Athens?
Frank Um . . . it's in Greece.
Lesley Yes! That's wonderful! And now the third question! Who is Michael Jackson?
Frank He's a singer!
Lesley That's correct! Open the doors! OK, Frank. Look for ten seconds!

Lesley Well, Frank, in thirty seconds . . . what is there on the table?
Frank Er . . . there's a telephone, um . . . a telephone and a table . . . and there are some glasses . . . and there are some suitcases. Oh! There's a tennis racket . . . Um, is there a typewriter?
Lesley No, there isn't a *typewriter* . . .
Frank Ooh, there's a computer!
Lesley Yes, it's a computer. It isn't a typewriter.
Frank Er . . . there are some books . . . some big books.
Lesley Yes, there are some dictionaries.
Frank Are there any knives and forks?
Lesley No, there aren't any knives and forks, but . . .
Frank Spoons! There are some silver spoons.
Lesley Yes, there are. Look at the time, Frank . . .
Frank Ooh! There's a clock! Um, a gold clock! Er, and golf clubs . . . Um, there's a coffee pot, a silver coffee pot, and a . . .
Lesley That's it! Look at your prizes, Frank!

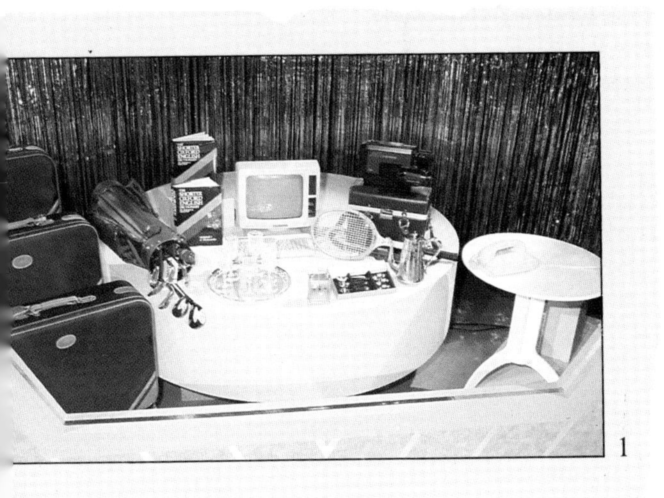
1

2

3

(a) Write a quiz

Here are some questions.

1 What is the capital of (Spain)?	*It's (Madrid).*
2 What is the language of (Turkey)?	*It's (Turkish).*
3 What nationality is (Stephen Spielberg)?	*He's (American).*
4 Where is (Milan)?	*It's in (Italy).*
5 Where is (Princess Diana) from?	*She's from (Britain).*
6 What colour is the (Japanese) flag?	*It's (red and white).*
7 Who is (Bruce Springsteen)?	*He's (a singer).*

Write seven *new* questions. Ask another student.

(b) Game

1 Student A: Look at picture two for thirty seconds. Close the book.
What is there in the picture?

2 Student B: Look at picture three for thirty seconds. Close the book.
What is there in the picture?

(c) Is there a briefcase?

A *Is there a briefcase in picture one?*
B *Yes, there is. / No, there isn't.*

A *Are there any spoons in picture one?*
B *Yes, there are. / No, there aren't.*

Ask and answer about the pictures.

(d) Write a list

Look at the three pictures. Write a list of ten things.

1	________	6	________
2	________	7	________
3	________	8	________
4	________	9	________
5	________	10	________

Ask about another student's list, with:

Is there a / an ______?
Yes, there's a / an ______.
No, there isn't a / an ______.

Are there any ______?
Yes, there are some ______.
No, there aren't any ______.

Is there any . . .?

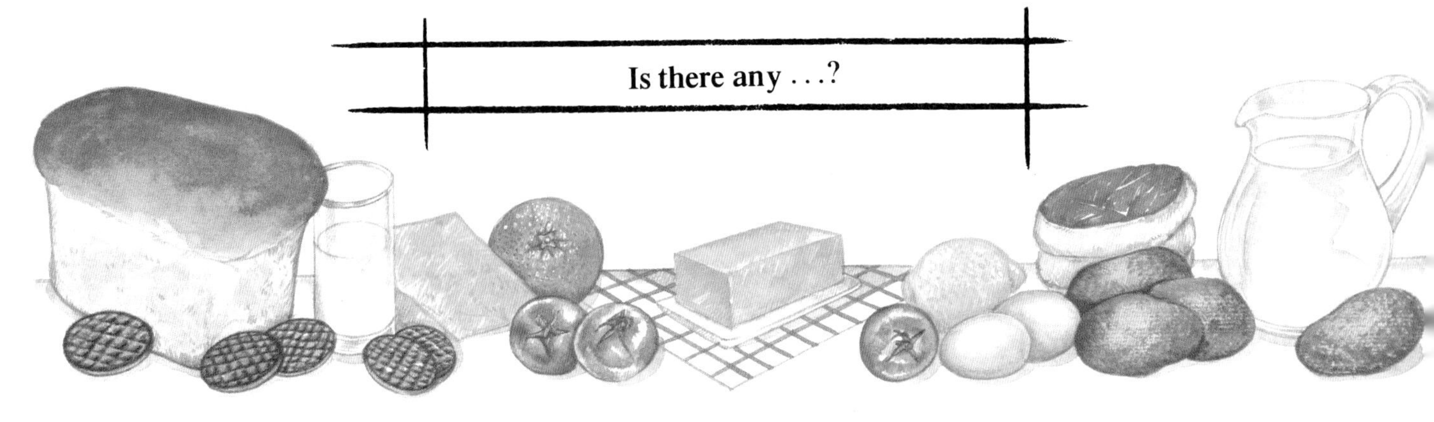

In English some things are **countable**, and some things are **uncountable**.

Countable

1 There's an orange in the picture.
2,3,4,5,6 . . . There are some tomatoes in the picture. / There are three tomatoes.

tomatoes **3** orange **1** apple **0**

Uncountable

There's some milk in the picture.

milk ✓ coffee 

a Chart

Look at the picture, and complete this chart.

potatoes 4	cheese ✓	eggs ______	lemon ______	biscuits ______
chicken ______	sandwich ______	water ______	meat ______	cola ______
tea ______	bread ______	butter ______	tuna ______	apple juice ______

b Is there a lemon?

A *Is there a lemon?*
B *Yes, there is. / No, there isn't.*
A *Are there any eggs?*
B *Yes, there are. / No, there aren't.*
A *Is there any milk?*
B *Yes, there is. / No, there isn't.*

Ask and answer about the picture above.

c True or false?

1 Look at the picture of breakfast.
Are these sentences true [✓] or false [✗]?

☐ There are two eggs on the plate.
☐ There's some tea in the jug.
☐ There are some cornflakes in the bowl.
☐ There isn't any bread on the plate.
☐ There isn't any milk in the bowl.
☐ There's some butter on the plate.

2 Student A: Write a *true or false?* exercise about lunch. Give it to Student B.
Student B: Write a *true or false?* exercise about tea. Give it to Student A.

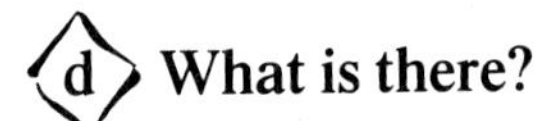

d What is there?

Look at **b Is there a lemon?**
Ask and answer about breakfast, lunch, and tea.

breakfast

lunch

tea

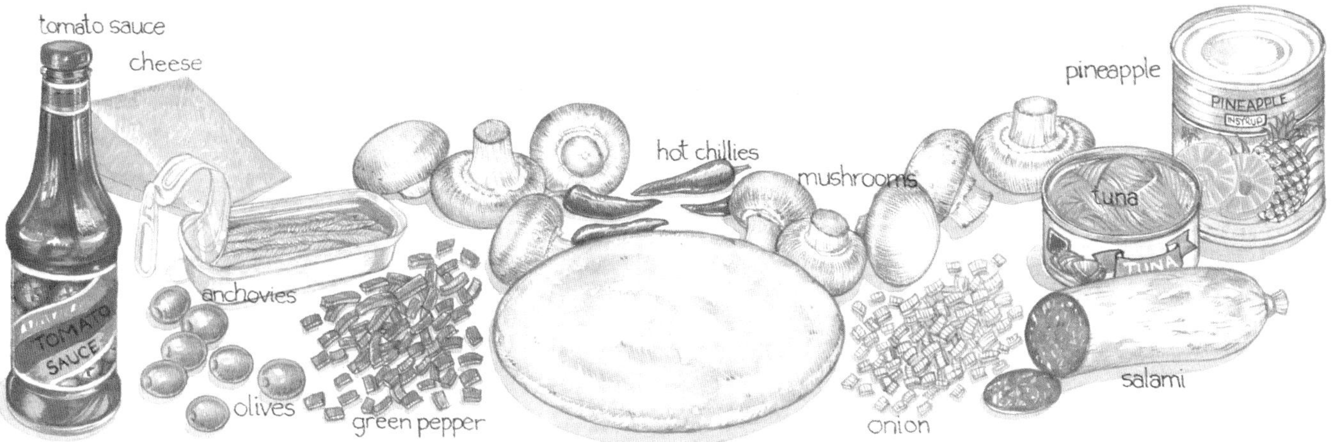

e The perfect pizza?

1 Look at the picture.
What things are countable? What things are uncountable? Make sentences about the picture with:
There's some . . . / There are some . . .

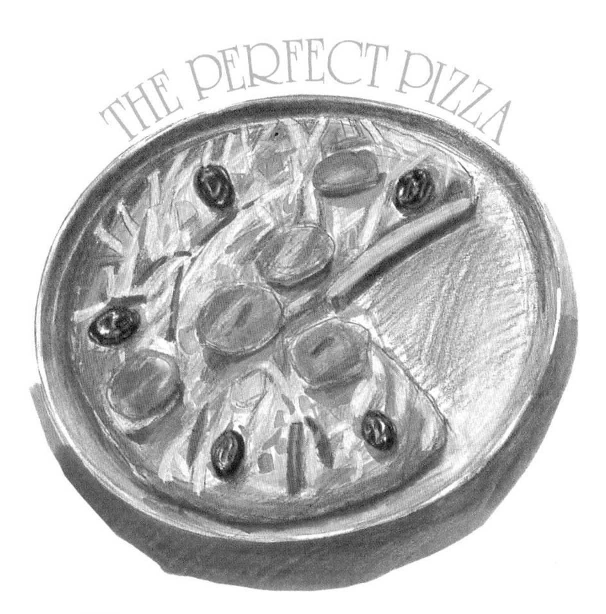

We deliver to your door - free!
Telephone us with your order!

Design your pizza

Large (35cm) Medium (25cm) Small (15cm)

A tomato and cheese pizza with:
• mushrooms • green pepper • onion • olives
• hot chillies • tuna • anchovies • salami
• pineapple

You choose!

Telephone: 156462
Open every day: 11.30 a.m. - Midnight

2 Look at the form. What is the perfect pizza for you?

3 Ask a student about his/her perfect pizza.

4 Role play. Telephone the pizza shop with your order.

f What's in the fridge?

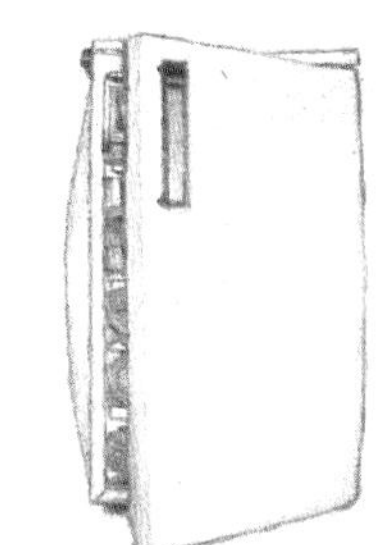

1 Guess what's in the fridge.
Write a list with five countable things and five uncountable things.

2 Now listen to the conversation about the fridge.
Put a tick [✓] by the things that are in the fridge and in your list

g News report

1 Listen to this news report.

Good evening, this is Gemma Walker for the six o'clock news. I'm in San Miguel. That's the volcano behind me. It's very bad here. There isn't any gas or electricity, and there isn't any clean water. There are five hundred people in the hospital, and there isn't any medicine there. There are some helicopters from the United States at the airport, and there's some food and there are some antibiotics on the helicopters. Our next report from San Miguel is at nine o'clock.

2 What's it like in San Miguel?
This is Gemma Walker's notebook:

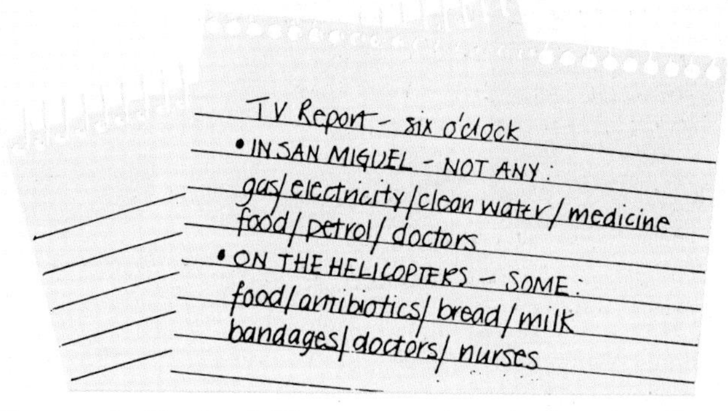

TV Report - six o'clock
• IN SAN MIGUEL - NOT ANY:
gas/electricity/clean water/medicine
food/petrol/doctors
• ON THE HELICOPTERS - SOME:
food/antibiotics/bread/milk
bandages/doctors/nurses

You are in England. You are on the telephone to Gemma.
Ask her about San Miguel.
Ask her about the helicopters.

The Family

TV NEWS 16th October

ETV's new television series, *The Family,* Wednesdays, 8.00 - 8.50

Meet The Family.

Donald Hewitt

Donald is a very rich man. He's got a computer factory in Cambridge. He's married to Rosemary. They've got three children, two sons and a daughter. He's got a house in Cambridge and a villa in Spain.

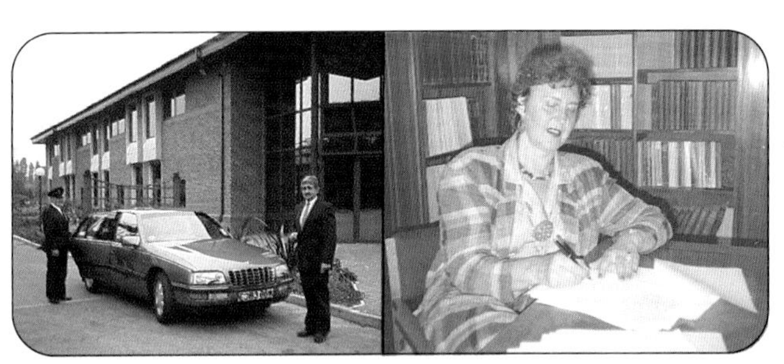

Rosemary Hewitt

Rosemary is Donald's wife. She's a writer of romantic novels, and she's very rich, too. She's got a flat in London, and she's got two cars, a Porsche and a Range Rover.

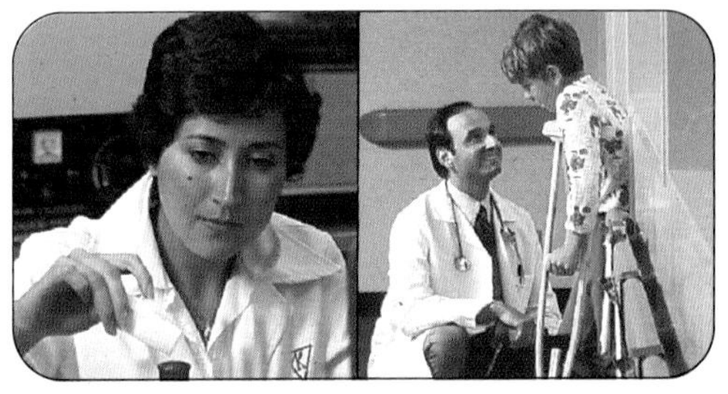

Charles & Amanda Hewitt

Charles is their son. He's 36. His wife's name is Amanda. They've got two children. Amanda's a famous model. Charles is a good businessman, but he isn't a nice person. He hasn't got any friends.

Andrea & Joseph Williams

Andrea is Donald and Rosemary's daughter. She's her father's favourite child. She's a scientist. Joseph is Andrea's husband. He's a doctor. Andrea's 32.

Robin Hewitt

Robin is Charles's and Andrea's brother. He's a rock singer, but he isn't famous. His father isn't happy about Robin's job. He hasn't got any money, and he hasn't got any children. He's 25. He's his mother's favourite child.

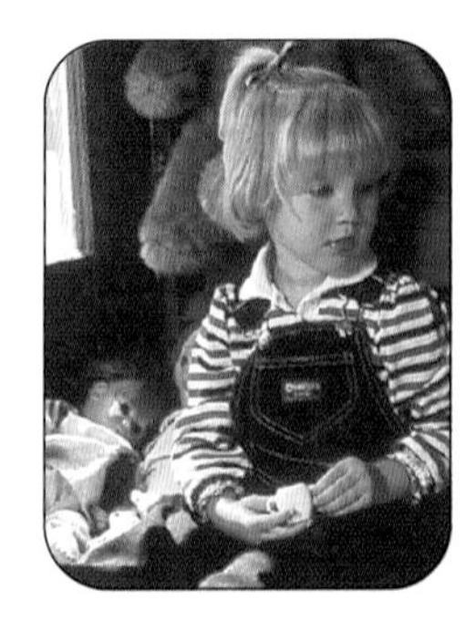

Lucy & David

They're Charles's children. Andrea is their aunt. Robin is their uncle. Lucy's Andrea's niece, and David's her nephew. Lucy is seven, and her brother is six. They've got two pets - a dog and a cat.

Peter & Claire

They're Lucy and David's cousins. They're Andrea's children. Peter's four, and his sister is two. Donald is their grandfather and Rosemary is their grandmother. They haven't got any pets.

The Family Competition

Win our fabulous first prize!
Dinner with the actors in
The Family at the ETV Studio!!!

Are these sentences true [✓] or false [✗] ?

- ☐ Donald is Robin's father.
- ☐ Peter is Charles's son.
- ☐ David is Robin's nephew.
- ☐ Charles is Claire's uncle.
- ☐ Andrea is Claire's aunt.
- ☐ Lucy is Andrea's niece.
- ☐ Andrea is Rosemary's daughter.
- ☐ Robin is Rosemary's grandson.
- ☐ Lucy is Donald's granddaughter.
- ☐ Andrea and Joseph are Peter's parents.
- ☐ Rosemary and Donald are Charles's grandparents.
- ☐ Amanda is Charles's wife.

Answer these questions about The Family.

1. Who is Rosemary's daughter?
2. Who are Rosemary's sons?
3. Who is Joseph's wife?
4. Who is Amanda's husband?
5. Who is Lucy's brother?
6. Who is Robin and Charles's sister?
7. Who are Charles's parents?
8. Who is Charles's niece?
9. Who are Robin's nephews?
10. Who are Peter's cousins?

Write your answers on a postcard, and send them to TV News. Watch the first programme for the address.

a Competition

Look at the competition.
Complete the *true or false* exercise, then ask and answer the questions.

b Family

Make more questions and answers with:

grandfather	son
grandmother	daughter
grandparents	grandson
parents	granddaughter
children	grandchildren
father	niece
mother	nephew
brother	uncle
sister	aunt
husband	cousin
wife	

c How old is she?

A *How old is Andrea?*
B *She's thirty-two.*
Ask and answer about the other people in 'The Family'.

d What's your favourite colour? Who's your favourite singer?

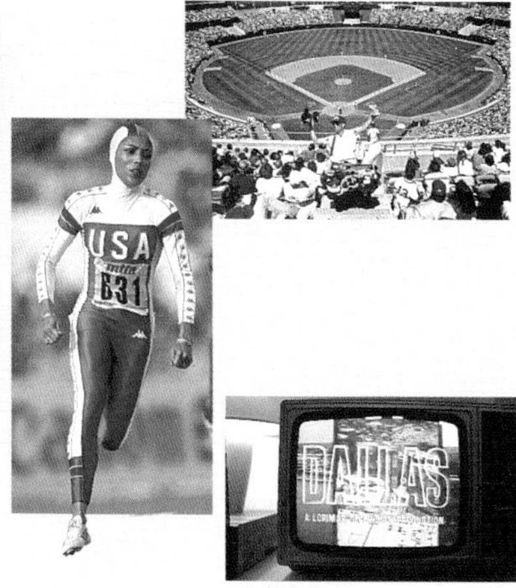

Have you got a favourite colour? What is it?
Have you got a favourite rock singer? Who is it?
Have you got a favourite sport? What is it?
Have you got a favourite sportsperson? Who is it?
Have you got a favourite TV programme? What is it?
Ask another student about his/her favourite people and things.

e Questionnaire

Ask another student questions with:
Have you got a . . . ? / Have you got any . . . ?

	Yes	No
brother(s)	☐	☐
sister(s)	☐	☐
cousin(s)	☐	☐
aunt(s)	☐	☐
uncle(s)	☐	☐

	Yes	No
pet(s)	☐	☐
house	☐	☐
flat	☐	☐
car	☐	☐

f About you and your partner

I've got two brothers.
I haven't got a sister. / I haven't got any sisters.
He's got five uncles.
She hasn't got any cousins.
Make sentences about you and your partner.

g About your family

A *Has your uncle got any children?*
B *Yes, he has. He's got six children.*
No. He hasn't got any children.

A *Has your mother got any brothers?*
B *Yes, she has. She's got one brother.*
No. She hasn't got any brothers.

A *Have your parents got a house?*
B *Yes, they have.*
No, they haven't. They've got a flat.

Ask and answer with another student.

People

The people at this party are all famous. Mrs Vincent is a cleaner. Mr Brown is a chauffeur. They're on the balcony.

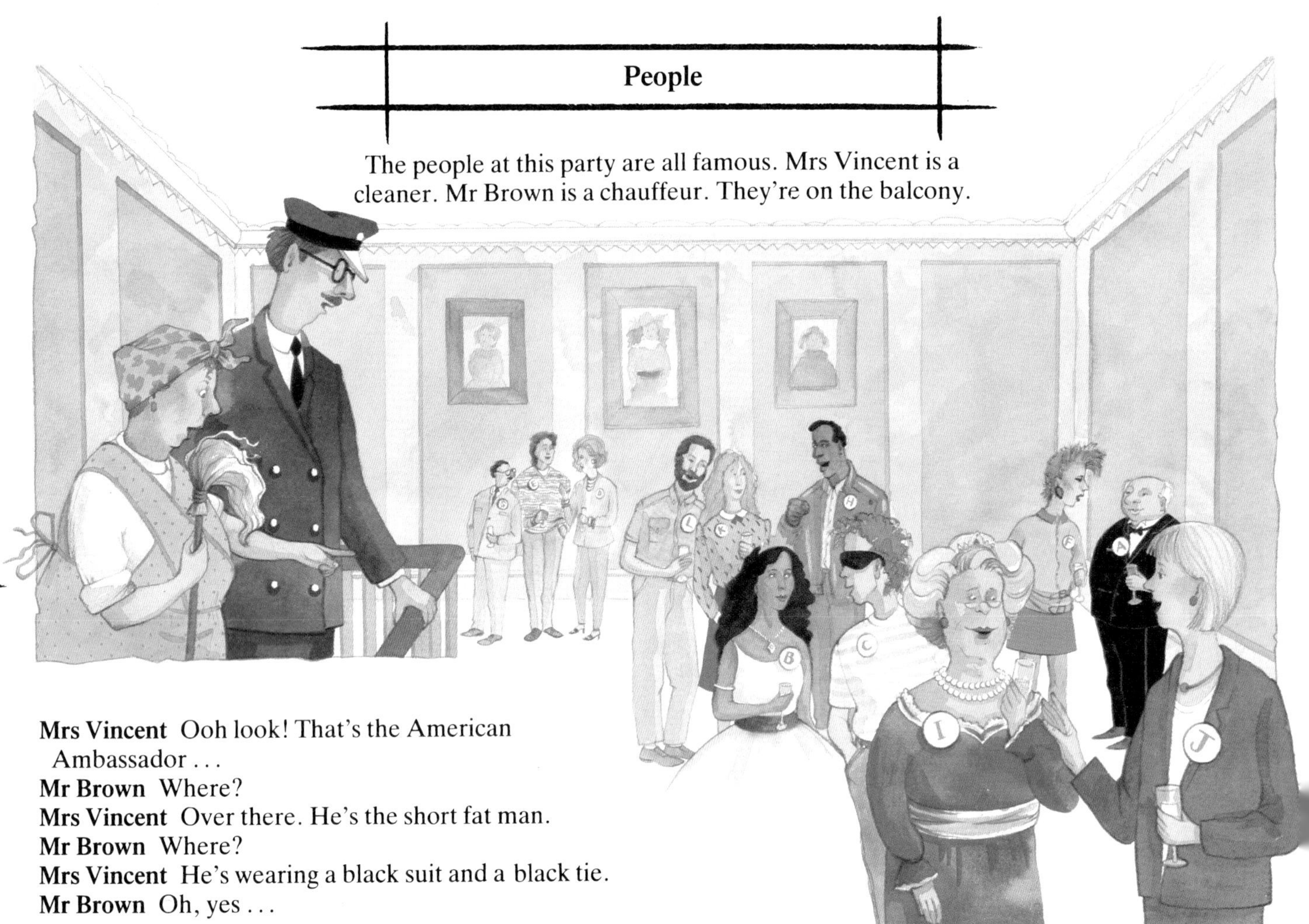

Mrs Vincent Ooh look! That's the American Ambassador . . .
Mr Brown Where?
Mrs Vincent Over there. He's the short fat man.
Mr Brown Where?
Mrs Vincent He's wearing a black suit and a black tie.
Mr Brown Oh, yes . . .

Mr Brown Who's she?
Mrs Vincent The woman with blond hair?
Mr Brown No. The tall woman over there. She's got dark hair.
Mrs Vincent Is she wearing a long white dress?
Mr Brown Yes, that's her.
Mrs Vincent That's Miss World! She's from Brazil.

Mrs Vincent Ooh! There's Michael George!
Mr Brown Where? What's he like?
Mrs Vincent He's next to Miss World. He's got red hair.
Mr Brown Oh, yes. He isn't wearing a suit!
Mrs Vincent But he's very good-looking.
Mr Brown Tut! He's wearing jeans . . . and a T-shirt. That's terrible. Who is he?
Mrs Vincent Don't you know? He's a singer. My daughter's got all his records.

Mrs Vincent There's Jean Collier! Oh, she's got lovely blond hair. Look, over there! She's wearing a pink trouser suit. She's about fifty, you know.
Mr Brown She's fifty-seven.
Mrs Vincent No! Really?
Mr Brown Yes. I'm her chauffeur.
Mrs Vincent Ooh! What's she like?
Mr Brown She's very nice.
Mrs Vincent Is she? Well, she's a wonderful actress.

a Who are they?

These are the people at the party.
Put the letters (A, B, C, . . .) in the spaces.

- [A] The American Ambassador. Short, fat. Black suit.
- [D] Jean Collier, actress. Blond hair. Pink trouser suit. About 50.
- [ ] Gary Trevor, footballer. Brown hair. Pullover. Good-looking.
- [ ] Donna, singer. Young. Orange and green hair. Skirt. Blouse.
- [ ] David Wilson, politician. Blue suit. Moustache. Middle-aged. Glasses.
- [ ] Doris Decker, tennis player. Long curly hair. About 27.
- [ ] Paul Cooper, racing driver. Brown hair. Beard. Green shirt. About 26.
- [ ] Barbara Heartland, writer. Old (87). Long dress. Blue hair. Glasses.
- [ ] Bruno Higgins, boxer. Black. Very tall. Pale blue shirt. Green trousers.
- [ ] Michael George, singer. Red hair. Jeans and T-shirt. Good-looking.
- [ ] Miss World. Tall. Long dark hair. White dress. Brazilian. Good-looking.
- [ ] Suzy Ford, newsreader. Average-height. About 35. Short blond hair.

b What are they like?

Ask and answer about the people at the party.

1 What's she like?

A *What's he / she like?*
B *She's tall / short / average-height.*
She's thin / fat / average-build.
He is / isn't good-looking.

2 How old is he?
A *How old is he / she?*
B *He's / she's young / old / middle-aged / about 20.*

3 What colour . . . ?

A *What colour is her hair?*
B *It's blond / dark / brown / black / red / grey.*
She's got (white) hair.

A *What colour are his eyes?*
B *They're blue / grey / green / brown.*
He's got (blue) eyes.

4 Has she got . . . ?

A *Has she got long / short / curly hair?*
B *Yes, she has. / No, she hasn't.*

A *Has he got glasses / a beard / a moustache?*
B *Yes, he has. / No, he hasn't.*

5 What is he wearing?

A *What is he wearing?*
B *He's wearing jeans / trousers / a suit / a shirt / a pullover / a T-shirt / a jacket.*

A *What is she wearing?*
B *She's wearing a dress / a skirt / a blouse / a trouser suit / blue shoes.*

c Who are they talking about?

Listen to these three people. They're talking about people at the party. Who are they talking about?

1 ______________________

2 ______________________

3 ______________________

d Describe them

Student A: Describe a person at the party.
Student B: Who is he/she talking about?

e Game

Student A: Describe a person in Units 1 to 12 or describe a person in the class.
Student B: Who is he/she talking about?

f

chorus:
There's tall thin Annie,
and short fat Dan.
She's his woman,
And he's her man.

She's got grey hair,
and her eyes are blue.
She's not good-looking,
And she's crazy, too.

chorus

He's got no hair,
and his eyes are brown
He's not good-looking,
with the face of a clown.

chorus

She's seventy-four,
He's eighty-five.
They're not good-looking,
but they're alive.

How much is it?

A Good morning.
B Good morning. Have you got a film for this camera, please?
A What size is it?
B 35 mm.
A 24 or 36-exposure?
B Er . . . 36, please.
A What make?
B Kodak, please. How much is it?
A £5.89.
B Thank you.

a Films

Make conversations.

Student A

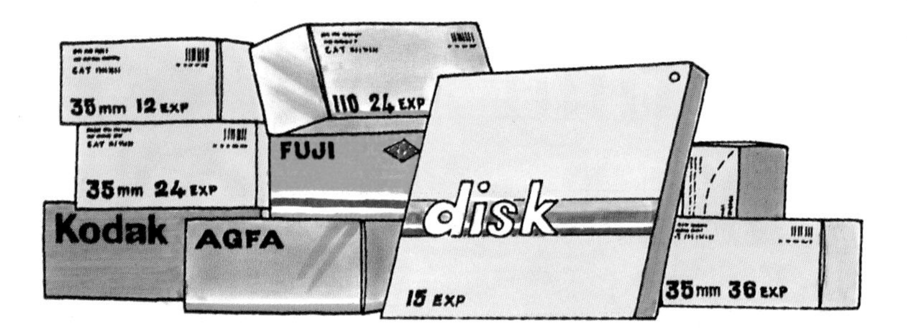

Student B

Prices

	110	disc	35mm		
	24 exp.	15 exp.	12 exp.	24 exp.	36 exp.
Fuji	2.95	1.95	2.20	4.05	5.59
Kodak	2.89	1.99	2.35	4.15	5.89
Agfa	2.75	1.75	2.50	3.99	5.49

C Yes, love?
D How much are the apples?
C 85p a pound.
D And have you got any grapes?
C Yes, love. Black or green?
D Black, please. How much are they?
C £1.60 a pound.
D Right. A pound of apples, and half a pound of grapes, please.
C There you are. That's £1.65 altogether.
D Thanks.

b Fruit

Make conversations.

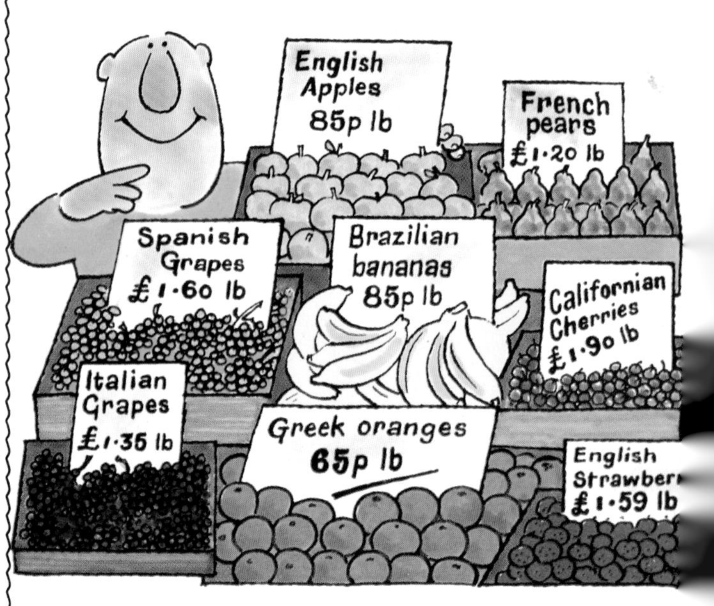

One pound (1 lb.) is 0.454 kilos.
Half a pound (1/2 lb.) is 0.227 kilos.
A quarter of a pound (1/4 lb.) is 0.114 kilos.

E Can I help you?
F Yes. How much is this pen, please?
E It's 40p.
F And how much are these postcards?
E They're 10p each.
F How much is the English tea?
E It's £1.20. Here you are.
F Oh, no. No, thank you. I'm just looking . . .

c Souvenirs

Make conversations.

Student A

this / that / the **these / those / the**

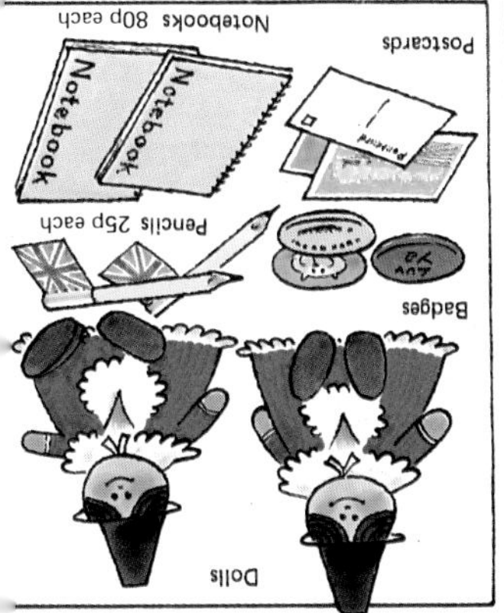

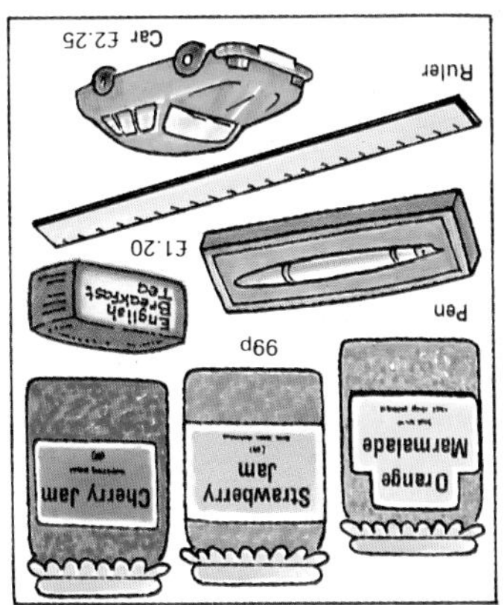

this / that / the **these / those / the**

Student B

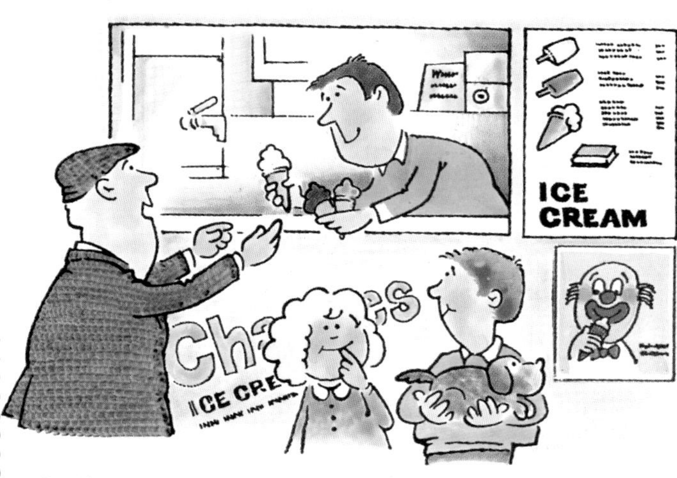

G Three small ice creams, please.
H What flavour?
G What flavours have you got?
H I've got strawberry, vanilla, chocolate, and coffee.
G OK, one strawberry, one vanilla, and one chocolate, please.
H Right . . . who's the strawberry for?
G It's for her.
H And the chocolate?
G It's for him. The vanilla's for me.
H Here you are.
G How much is that?
H They're 60p each . . . that's £1.80 altogether.

d Ice creams

Make conversations.

The Keys

1
Ben There's a programme on television!
Sarah Don't turn on the television, Ben.

4
Sarah Oh no . . . Ben! Ben, come here. Turn off the television, Ben. Ben, turn off the television and come here . . . Ben, open this door. Ben. Ben, please!

5
Postman What's wrong?
Sarah It's my little boy. He's inside, and my keys are in there. And the door's locked.
Postman Oh dear. Oh dear. Oh dear.

6
Postman How old is he?
Sarah He's four.
Postman What about the back door?
Sarah That's locked, too.

7
Postman And the windows? Have you got a ladder?
Sarah No, I haven't. Wait here a minute . . .

8a 8b
Postman Hello? Hello?
Sarah Be quiet! Bad dog! Be quiet! Don't do that! Sit! Sit! . . . Sorry.

9
Mrs Clark Be careful, dear.
Mr Clark Oh, I'm all right.
Mrs Clark Not you, dear. The garden. Be careful.

10
Sarah Please be careful, Mr Clark.
Mr Clark I'm OK. Help me. Hold the ladder.
Postman OK.

11
Mr Clark It's a very small window.
Postman Put your hand in!
Mr Clark Eh?
Postman Put your hand in! Pull the handle!
Mr Clark What?

12
Postman Pull the handle of the other window.
Mr Clark Oh.
Postman Pull the handle!
Mr Clark It's no good!

13
Sarah Ben! Turn off the television! *Ben! Come here!*
Ben Hello, Mum.

14
Sarah Ben, the door's locked, and I haven't got my keys. Open the door. It's no good. He's very small, you see.
Mrs Clark Oh dear. Oh dear, oh dear.

15
Sarah Right, Ben. Get my bag. It's in the hall. Have you got it?
Ben Yes.
Sarah Open my bag . . . and get the purse. Open it. The keys are in the purse. Have you got them?
Ben Yes.

16
Sarah Good boy. Now, come here, and push the keys through the letter-box. Oh no! These are the car keys!

17

Sarah Ben, don't go. Come here. Come here, Ben! Don't turn on the television. These aren't the house keys. They're the car keys.

18

Sarah Get the purse. Get mummy's purse. Now push the purse through the letter-box. Push! Push!
Postman Pull!
Sarah Thank you.

19

Ben Push!
Sarah Ben, don't do that! Don't put the purse through the letter-box! Ben!

a Role play

In groups of four, role play the story of the keys.

Come here.
Open the window!
Pull it!
Turn the TV off!
Be quiet!
Don't go there!
Don't open the door!
Don't push it!
Don't turn it on!
Be careful!

b Instructions

Listen. Get up. Get a chair. Put it on the table. Get a book. Put it on the chair. Get a pen. Put it on the book. Go to the door. Push the door. / Pull the door. Open it. Go out. Close the door. Open the door. Come in. Come here. Don't move. Be quiet.

Listen. Get up. Turn on the light. Go to the cassette player. Turn it on. Don't move. Turn it off. Go to the light. Turn it off. Get a chair. Stand on the chair. Be careful. Get on the table. Get off the table. Come here.

Look at the instructions. Give some instructions to another student.

c What?

Look at the pictures. Complete the spaces.

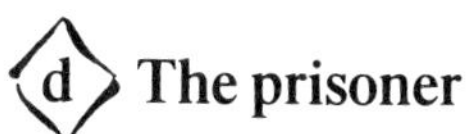

d The prisoner

This man is a prisoner in this room. The door is locked. The man has got a pen and some paper. Help him to get out. Give instructions.

Answer

Get the paper. Push the paper under the door. Get the pen. Push the pen into the lock. Push the key with the pen. Pull the paper under the door. The key is on the paper!

Security

Bert Ellis is 66. He's retired, but he isn't happy. He's looking for another job.

JOBS

WAITER for small but busy restaurant. 40-hour week. Chelsea. 01-447- 9855.

NIGHT SECURITY GUARD for large insurance company. City of London. 5 nights per week. 10 pm to 6 am. Tel: Ms J Cooper, Personnel Manager, 01-243-9088.

VAN DRIVER East London. 42-hour week. Good salary. Clean driving licence essential. Call Tim on 01-554-3361.

The next day.

Monday 11.00 p.m. The offices of Mercia Insurance. Bert is with the other security guard, Dave. Dave is 29.

SECURITY GUARD HERO gets the wrong man - but he keeps his job!

'He's a very brave man' says company boss Ernest Miles. Mr Miles is in our photograph with 66 year-old security guard, Bert Ellis, from Hackney. Bert, who started work with M

Directions

A Can I help you?
B Yes. I'm looking for a map of the town.
A There are some maps over here. This is a good one.
B How much is it?
A £1.35.
B That's fine. Thank you.

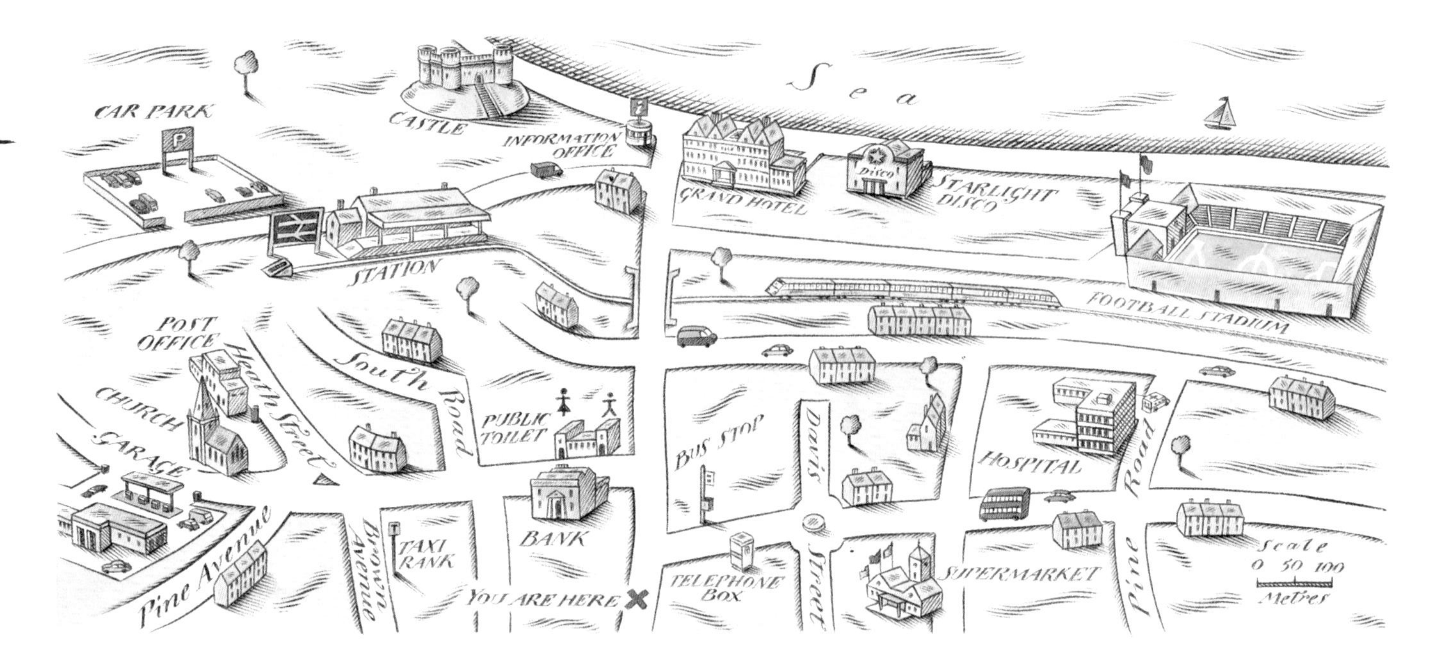

(a) Asking the way

1 **C** Excuse me, where's Heath Street?
D It's first left, then second right.
C Thank you.

Make conversations for:
Brown Avenue / Davis Street / South Road / Pine Road.

2 **E** Excuse me, is there a bus stop near here?
F Yes. Go along this street, turn right and it's on the left.

Make conversations for:
a public toilet / a telephone box / a bank.

3 **G** Excuse me, I'm looking for a post office.
H Go along this street, take the first left, then the second right. It's on the left. You can't miss it.
G Thank you very much.
H Not at all.

Make conversations for:
a supermarket / a hospital / a taxi rank.

4 **I** Excuse me, can you tell me the way to the Grand Hotel?
J Yes, go along this street. Go across the bridge and go straight on to the end. It's on the right at the end of the street.

Make conversations for:
the football stadium / the information office / the station.

5 **K** Excuse me, I'm looking for a garage.
L A garage? Yes, go along this street, and turn first left. Go straight on for about 400 metres. Go past the church, and it's on the left.
K Thanks.

Make conversations for:
The Starlight Disco / a car park / the Castle.

M Excuse me, can you tell me the way to the Castle?
N Sorry, I don't know. I'm a stranger here.

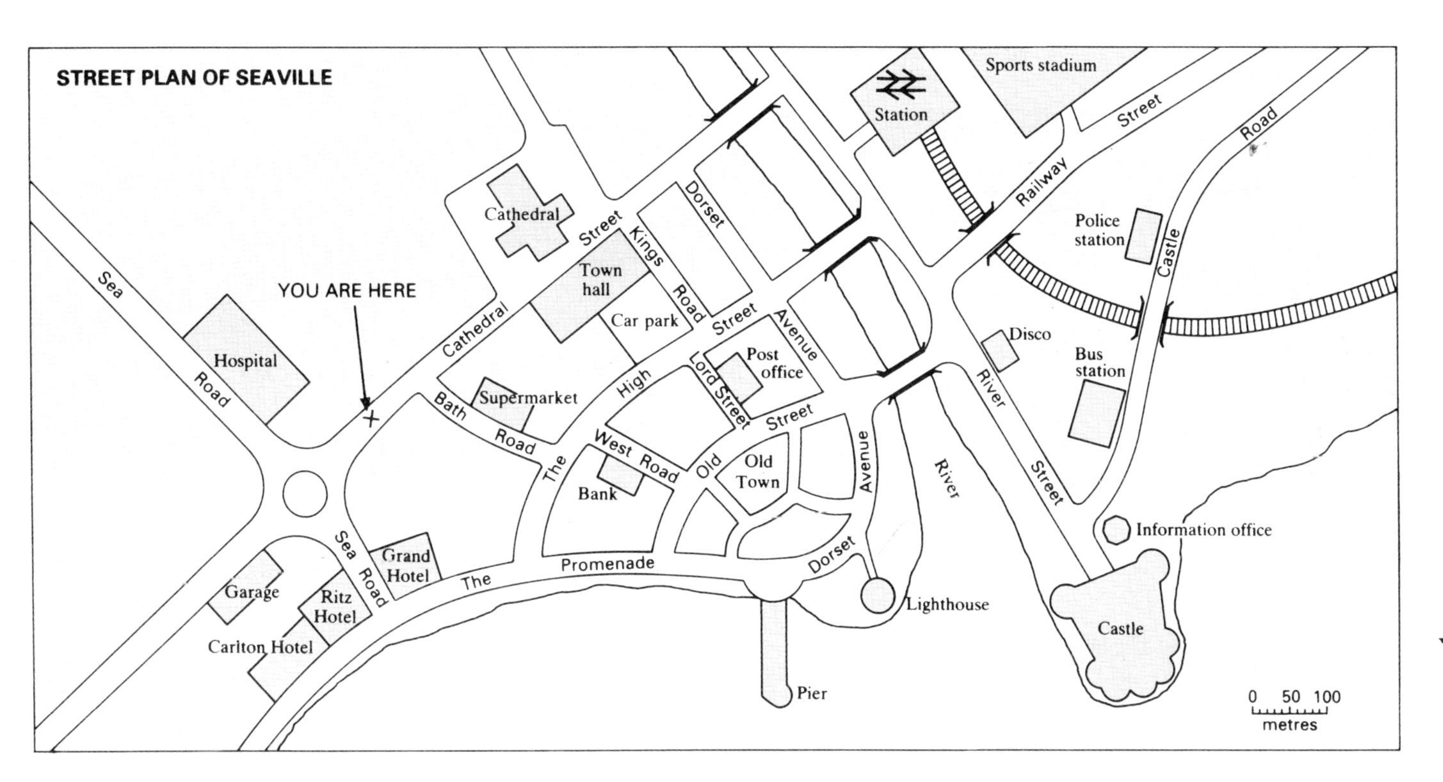

b Seaville

1. You are in Cathedral Street.
   Listen to these four people, and put 1, 2, 3, and 4 on the map.
2. Asking the way in Seaville.
   Student A: Ask the way to the police station / the Ritz Hotel / the lighthouse / the post office.
   Student B: Look at the map.
   Tell your partner the way.

c Directions game

Student A: Look at the maps.
Give Student B directions to a place on a map.
Student B: What is the place?

d Computer game

Where is the gold?
Student A: Tell Student B the way to the gold.
Student B: Tell Student A the way to the exit.

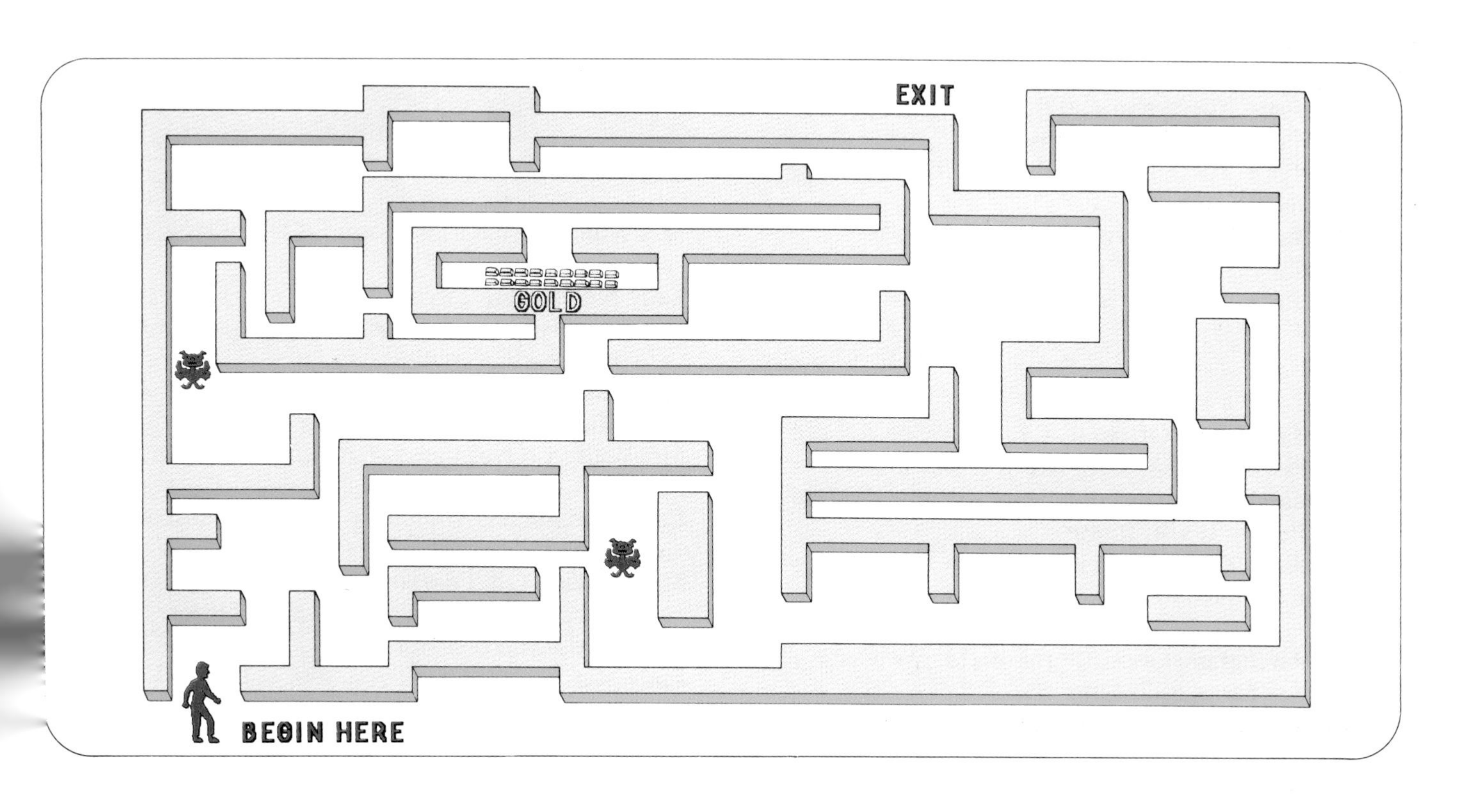

Marchmain Castle

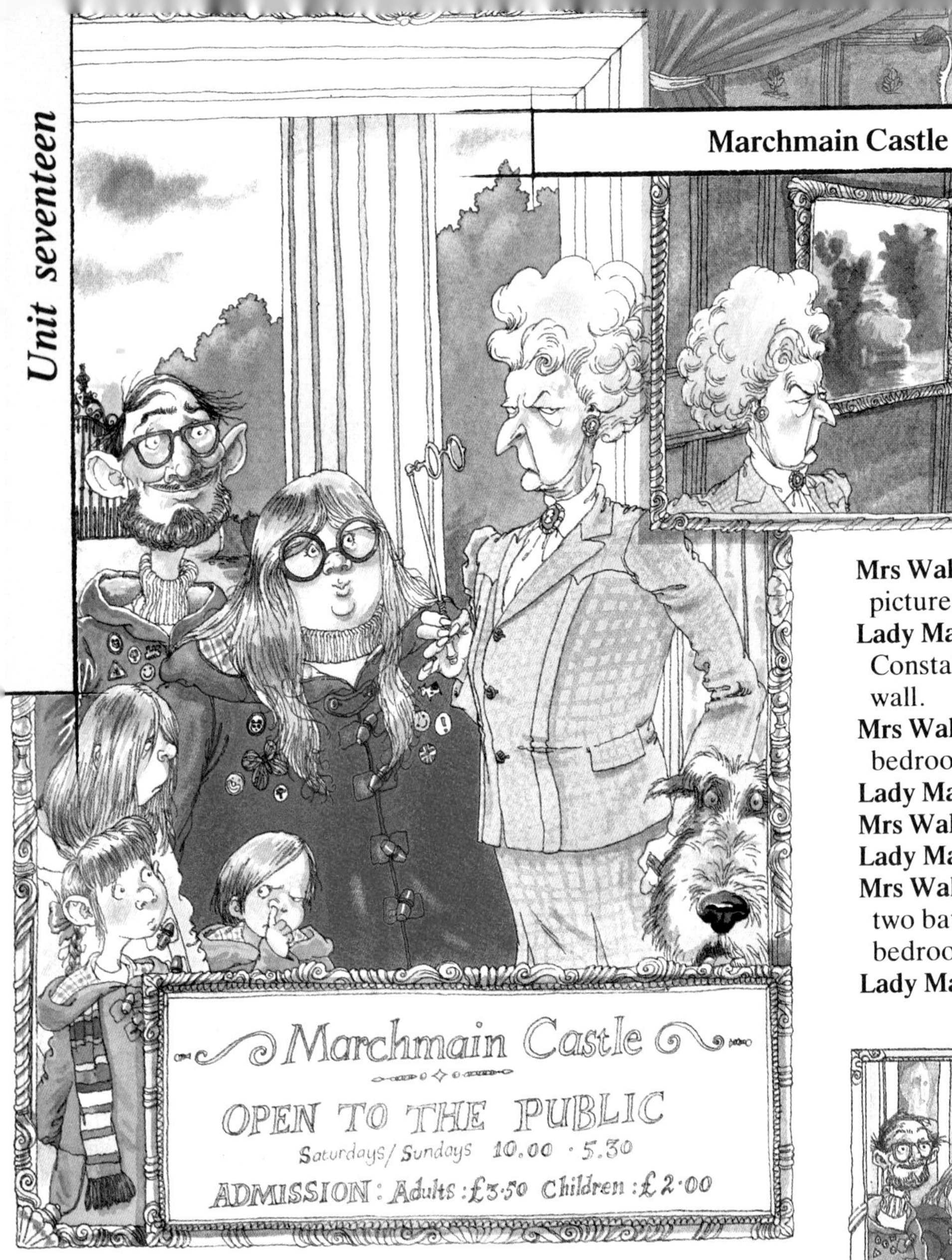

Lady Marchmain Yes?
Mr Wallace Two adults and three children, please.
Lady Marchmain I beg your pardon?
Mr Wallace Two adults and three children, please. How much is that?
Lady Marchmain I'm sorry. It's 5.45 p.m. We're closed.
Mr Wallace Oh, dear. Sorry, kids. They're closed.

Lady Marchmain Oh, well ... er, come in.
Mr Wallace Thanks, love. Are you the guide?
Lady Marchmain The guide? No, I'm not. I'm Lady Marchmain. It's my house.
Mr Wallace Oh! Pleased to meet you. My name's Wallace. Malcolm Wallace ... and this is my wife, Jean.
Lady Marchmain Good afternoon, Mr Wallace ... Mrs Wallace. Er ... follow me.

Mrs Wallace Oh, it's very nice! You've got some lovely pictures!
Lady Marchmain Yes ... there are three paintings by Constable over there, and two Rembrandts on this wall.
Mrs Wallace It's a very big house. How many bedrooms are there?
Lady Marchmain There are eighteen bedrooms.
Mrs Wallace And how many bathrooms?
Lady Marchmain There are two bathrooms.
Mrs Wallace Oh! There aren't very many! We've got two bathrooms in our house, and we've only got three bedrooms!
Lady Marchmain Yes ... well, it's a very old house.

Mrs Wallace That's an enormous table! How many chairs are there?
Lady Marchmain Twenty-four. We've got two dining rooms, this one and our private dining room. There are only six chairs in that one.
Mrs Wallace Oh! What's that?
Lady Marchmain Where?
Mrs Wallace Over there ... in the chair! It's a dead body!
Lady Marchmain No, it isn't. That's my husband, Lord Marchmain. He's asleep.
Mrs Wallace Oh, I *am* sorry. Well, thank you Lady Marchmain. Er ... We're from Manchester. If you're there, come and see our house!
Lady Marchmain Thank you. Oh ... that's £13.
Mrs Wallace Pardon?
Lady Marchmain £13 ... for the tickets.

Famous Houses of Britain: Vol 5: The North

YORKSHIRE

Marchmain Castle
Marchthorpe, Yorkshire. Tel: Marchthorpe 3259
Shipton – 3m. York – 9m. Selby –19m. Leeds – 28m.
Hull – 35m. Manchester – 70m.

Directions
Car: A19 from York, turn right at Shipton.
Bus: Number 14 from York.
Train: To York, then bus or taxi.
There is a large car park (200 cars).
Walk out of the car park, and go across the small bridge.
The ticket office is on the left.

Admission
Open: Saturdays / Sundays 10.00 - 5.30
Closed on weekdays, bank holidays.
Tickets: Adults £3.50, Children £2.00, Students £2.50

Restaurant
Self-service cafeteria next to the house. Lunches, snacks, teas.

Souvenir shop
Behind the cafeteria.

Information
Beautiful house designed by Charles Adams (1635) in lovely gardens. 18 bedrooms. Home of the Marchmain family for 300 years. Many famous paintings - look for two Rembrandts, three Constables, four Turners, two Leonardos, five Van Eykes. Collection of vintage cars (1896 - 1914) in the garages.

a Guidebook

Look at the information about Marchmain Castle.

1 Put a tick [✓] in the correct box below.

	Yes	No
1 Is the house open at 9.00 in the morning?	☐	☐
2 Is the phone number Marchthorpe 3259?	☐	☐
3 Are students' tickets £2.50 each?	☐	☐
4 Is the ticket office on the right?	☐	☐
5 Is the cafeteria in the house?	☐	☐
6 Is the house open on Sundays?	☐	☐
7 Is the bus from York number 41?	☐	☐
8 Are there two paintings by Leonardo in the house?	☐	☐

2 How many?

A *How many miles is the house from York?*
B *It's nine miles from York.*

A *How many paintings are there by Rembrandt?*
B *There are two paintings by Rembrandt.*

Ask and answer about Marchmain Castle.

3 Student A: Look at the guidebook.
Student B: Close the book and ask about Marchmain Castle.

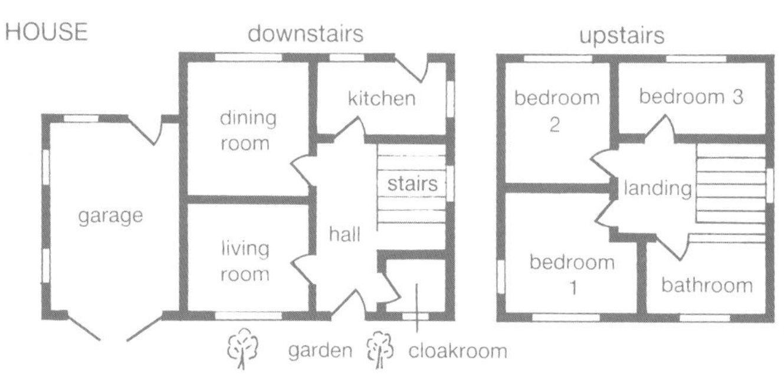

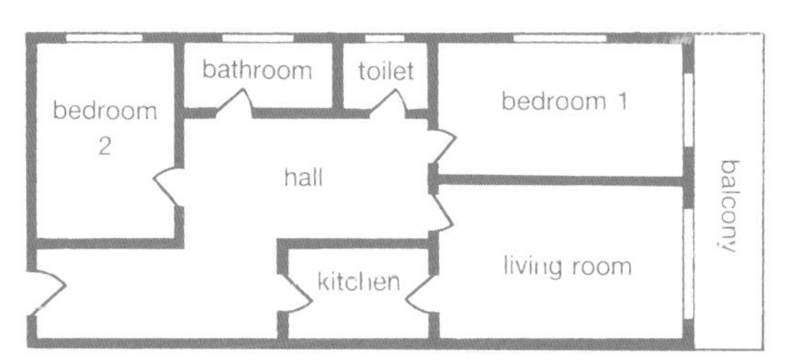

b Houses and flats

How many rooms / bedrooms are there?
How many rooms are there upstairs / downstairs?
How many doors / windows / toilets are there?

Ask and answer about the house, the flat, your house or flat, and your bedroom.

c How many have you got?

A *How many brothers have you got?*
B *I've got two brothers. / I haven't got any brothers.*

Ask two students questions and complete the questionnaire.

	Student 1	Student 2
Family		
brothers		
sisters		
uncles		
aunts		
cousins		
grandparents		
Things		
records / cassettes		
English books		
belts		
pullovers / cardigans		
? (you make the question)		

d How many has she got?

Work with a different student.
A *How many brothers has he / she got?*
B *He's got two brothers. / She hasn't got any brothers.*

Talk about the other students in your class.

It's mine!

Sorry!

Man Sorry! Er . . . whose glasses are these?
Old lady They're mine . . . thank you.
Man Is this yours?
Old lady The baby food? No, that isn't mine . . .
Woman It's ours. Thanks.

a Whose is it?/Whose are they?

A *Whose glasses are those? / Whose are the glasses?*
B *They're his / hers / theirs.*

A *Whose baby food is that? / Whose is the baby food?*
B *It's his / hers / theirs.*

Ask and answer about the things on the supermarket floor.

Susan Hello, Mr Dodds. Is that bag heavy?
Mr Dodds Hello, Susan. Well, yes, it is.
Susan My car's over there. Come on, come with me . . .
Mr Dodds That's very kind of you. Thank you.
Susan That's my car . . . over there.
Mr Dodds Which one? The white one? It's very nice.
Susan No! That's mine next to it. It's the black one!

b Which one?

Work in groups of five or six. The group has got a bag.
Each student puts three or four things in the bag.
The other students don't look.
Put all the things on the floor.

A *Whose is this pen?*
Is this pen yours?
B *It isn't mine.*
It's hers.
It's Maria's.

A *Which pen is yours?*
Which one is hers?
B *The blue one's mine.*
The old one's hers.

Ask and answer about the things.

c Which ones?

Look at the trousers.

A *Which ones are his?*
Which trousers are his?
B *The blue ones are his.*

Ask and answer about the picture.

d Encyclopaedia

Vol 1	Vol 2	Vol 3	Vol 4	Vol 5	Vol 6
Abacus - Aztec	Baby - Car	Carbon - Czech	Daimler - France	Frankenstein - Hospital	Hotel - Krakatoa

Vol 7	Vol 8	Vol 9	Vol 10	Vol 11	Vol 12
Kremlin - Medicine	Mediterranean - Oxygen	Pacific - Reading	Reagan - Star	State - Typhoid	Typhoon - Zurich

Look at this 12-volume encyclopaedia.
1 You are looking for information in the encyclopaedia. Which volumes are these words in?

__ television	__ St. Peter	__ Mexico
__ computers	__ fishing	__ London
__ driving	__ The Beatles	__ Queen Anne
__ kangaroo	__ Mozart	__ The Nile
__ Hemingway	__ agriculture	__ The USSR
__ physics	__ jazz	__ Napoleon

2 Work with your partner.

A *Which volume is (Einstein) in?*
B *It's in volume (four).*

Ask about other words.

Asking for things

In a record shop

A Yes?
B I'd like *Sixteen Greatest Hits* by Cyndi Lawson, please.
A Would you like the LP, the cassette, or the compact disc?
B Oh, sorry. I'd like the cassette, please.
A That's £6.89.
B Thank you.

1. **Sixteen Greatest Hits**
   Cyndi Lawson (Pacific)
2. **How many tears?**
   4 U (Shamrock)
3. **Karate King 5** (Film soundtrack)
   Mario Marietti (Korner Brothers)
4. **Happy or Sad**
   The plugs (BCS)
5. **Smash, Crash, Bang**
   Titanium (Polygon)
6. **You wouldn't tell me**
   Angie Dallas (Pacific)
7. **West Texas Child**
   Carl Lee Hoover (BCS)
8. **2095**
   The Duke (IEA)
9. **On stage**
   The Earrings (Pink Punk)
10. **The Island**
    Cyndi Lawson (Pacific)

a The Top Ten

Ask and answer.

1 Which record is number four this week?
2 How many Pacific records are in the Top Ten?
3 How many records has Cyndi Lawson got in the Top Ten?
4 Whose record is number eight this week?
5 Which group is *Smash, Crash, Bang* by?
6 Who is *West Texas Child* by?

Inland Letters and Cards

	60g	100g	150g	200g
1st Class	19p	28p	34p	42p
2nd Class	14p	22p	26p	32p

Overseas Letters (Air)

Zone A (N Africa, Middle East)	30p (10g)
Zone B (Americas, Africa, India, SE Asia)	32p (10g)
Zone C (Australasia, Japan, China)	35p (10g)
Europe (EEC countries)	19p (20g)
Europe (non-EEC) and surface letters	23p (20g)

Please use the postcode and include a return address.

Promoter:
Royal Mail, Room 194A, 33 Grosvenor Place, LONDON SW1X 1PX

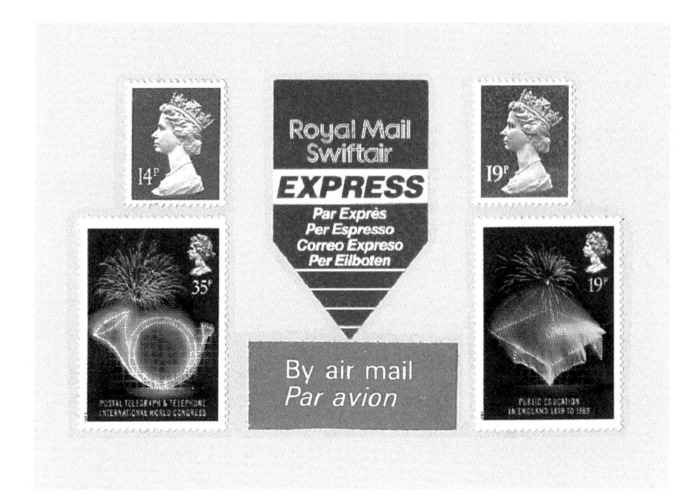

In the post office

E I'd like some stamps, please.
F How many?
E I'd like two first class, and one for this airmail letter.
F Where's it going to?
E The United States.
F Put it on the scales, please. Mmm, that's 32p, and two nineteens. That's 70p altogether.
E Thanks.
F Would you like an airmail sticker?
E Yes, I would. Thank you.

b Book of stamps

1 Find abbreviations for:
____gram ____European Economic Community
____pence ____South-East ____North.

2 How much is a stamp for a 10-gram letter to:
____Japan ____The USA ____Saudi Arabia
____France ____Mexico ____Czechoslovakia?

c One of those

Make conversations.

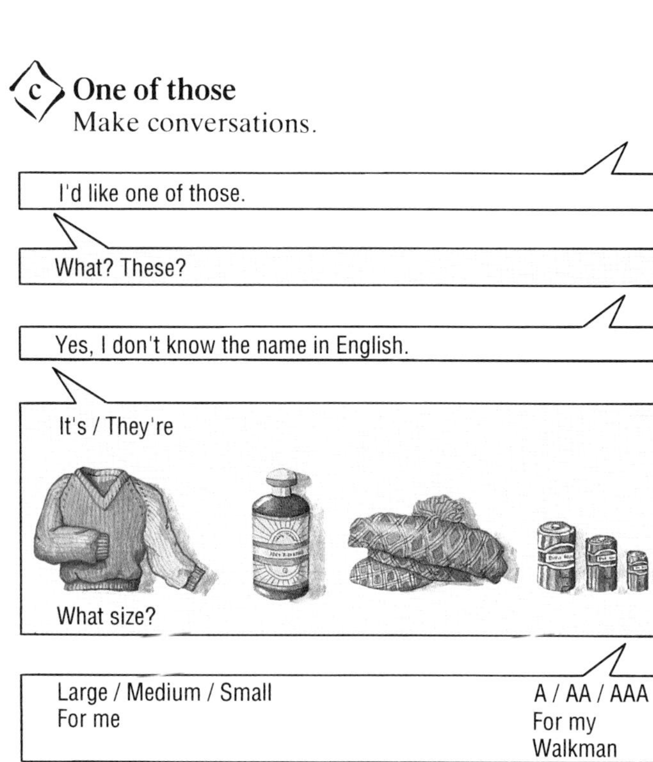

d What's its name in English?

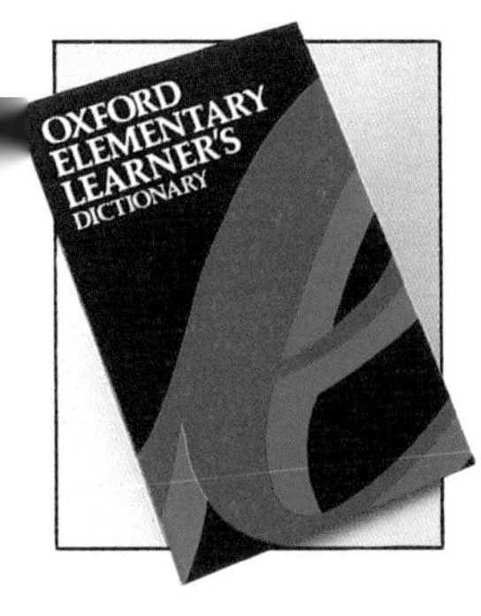

battery /'bætərɪ/ *n.* (*pl.* batteries) group of cells in a container which give electricity: *I put a new battery into my radio.*

suntan /'sʌntæn/ *n.* brown colour of your skin when you have been in the hot sun. **suntanned** /'sʌntænd/ *adj.*

lotion /'ləʊʃn/ *n.* soft liquid that you put on the skin: *suntan lotion.*

pullover /'pʊləʊvə(r)/ *n.* jersey; sweater.

cap /kæp/ *n.* **1** sort of soft hat. **2** cover for the top of a tube, bottle, etc.

Student A: Read about something in a dictionary. Describe it to Student B.
Student B: What's its name in English? Guess.

e What size?

Put things from column 1 with things from column 2.

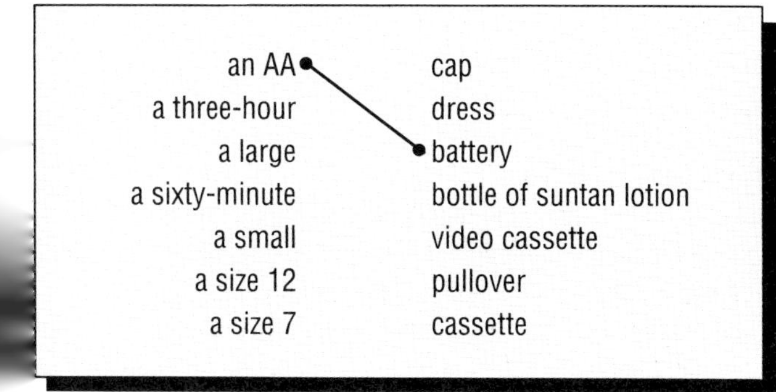

f A two-hour cassette

Video cassettes: E120 E180 E240
Cassettes: C30 C60 C90 C120
(An E120 is a two-hour video cassette – **not** two-hours.)
(A C30 is a thirty-minute cassette, etc.)

A *I'd like a two-hour video cassette, please.*
B *Ah, yes. That's an E120.*
Make more conversations.

g Role play

Student A is the customer in a clothes shop and is looking for a present. Student B is the shop assistant. Look at the boxes, and have a conversation.

Student A

Colours	*Red, blue, green, yellow, brown, grey dark blue, light blue*, etc.
Sizes	*Large, medium, small* or *size 12, size 36*, etc.
Make	*Benneton, Lacoste*, etc.
Who for ?	*Boyfriend / girlfriend, aunt, grandfather, mother, brother*, etc.

Student B

Which colour would you like?
What size would you like?
What make would you like?
Who is it for?

Chips with everything

Lunch

Listen to the conversation in the restaurant. Number the pictures from 1 to 8.

Martin Excuse me, we'd like a table for two, please.
Waiter Well, I don't know . . . we're very busy at lunchtime.
Martin Is this table free?
Waiter Well . . . yes.
Martin Could we have the menu, please? We're in a hurry.
Waiter Here you are.

Martin Ah, soup. What would you like, darling? They've got tomato or minestrone.
Angela Mmm . . . I'd like the tomato soup. What about the main course?
Martin Oh, I'd like the steak. And you?
Angela Yes, the steak for me, too. And a salad. Not chips.

Martin Excuse me!
Waiter Yes, sir?
Martin We'd like two tomato soups, please.
Waiter Tomato soup's off the menu. We haven't got any.
Angela Could we have two minestrone soups, then?
Waiter Minestrone's off, too.
Angela What *have* you got?
Waiter We've got soup of the day.
Angela What is it?
Waiter Um . . . potato . . .
Angela All right. Two potato soups, then.
Waiter Two . . . potato . . . soups. Anything else?
Martin Yes. We'd like two steaks, please. One rare, and one well-done.
Waiter Steak's off. We haven't got any.
Martin All right. Could we have two chicken, please?
Waiter Chicken's off.
Martin I see. Have you got any fish?
Waiter Uh, uh.

Martin What have you got?
Waiter Egg and chips, hot dog and chips, sausage and chips, hamburger and chips, spaghetti . . .
Martin And chips?
Waiter . . . Bolognese. Spaghetti Bolognese.
Angela All right. Two spaghetti Bolognese, then . . . and a salad.

Waiter A salad?
Angela Yes, I'd like a salad.
Waiter You wouldn't.
Angela I would.
Martin She would. What's wrong with that?
Angela You're right. I wouldn't.

Martin Your finger's in my soup.
Waiter It's all right, sir. It isn't hot.
Angela That's it! Come on, Martin.
Waiter Hey! What about your spaghetti? Probably not hungry.

Old England Restaurant

MENU

STARTERS

1 *Tomato soup* £1.20
2 *Soup of the day* £0.95
3 *Minestrone soup* £1.30
4 *Melon* £1.95

MAIN COURSES

(All served with chips and peas)

5 *Steak* £6.95
6 *Chicken* £5.95
7 *Fish* £4.95
8 *Two hamburgers* £3.95
9 *Sausages* £2.95
10 *Two eggs* £2.35
11 *Hot dog* £2.55
12 *Spaghetti Bolognese* £3.50
13 *Side salad* £1.50

DESSERTS

14 *Ice cream* £1.20
(strawberry, chocolate, vanilla)
15 *Apple pie* £1.30
16 *Fruit salad* £1.40

SERVICE 10% VAT AT 15% INCLUDED

b Dinner

Listen to these three customers in the Old England Restaurant.
Write their orders on the chart below.
Write the numbers from the menu (e.g. for **chicken** write **6**).

	Starter	Main course	Dessert
1			
2			
3			

c A table for two

Complete the conversation.

Waiter Good evening, ______ .
You Good evening. ______ a table for two, please.
Waiter Here you are, ______ . This is a nice table.
You Thank you. ______ a menu, please?
Waiter Here you are. Would ______ a starter?
You Yes. ______ for me, and ______ for ______ .
Waiter And ______ main course?
You Please. I ______ , and ______ 'd ______ .
Waiter Right. Anything ______ , ______ ?
You Yes. We'd like desserts. Could ______ and ______ .
Waiter Is that all, ______ ?
You Yes. Thank you.

d Role play

1 Look at the menu. Make conversations in pairs. Student A is the waiter / waitress. Student B is the customer.

2 Look at the menu. There are two (or three) customers and a waiter in the restaurant. Make conversations in a group of three or four.

Mickey can't dance

MUSIC MAIL

Meet Independence Day

The number three record this week is *Mickey can't dance,* a song from the album 'This is Independence Day'. But who are Independence Day?
Independence Day are an international group of disabled musicians. They are all in wheelchairs. Paul Thomson is from London. He's 20. He's the guitarist and singer, and he can also play the piano. Jill Raymond, from Canada, is the bass guitarist. She can also sing and play the saxophone. She's 19. Five of the songs on the album, 'This is Independence Day', are by Paul and Jill, including their first hit, *Mickey can't dance.*
Denise Cooper is the keyboard player. She can play the piano, synthesizer, and organ. She's 21, and she's from New Zealand. Julian Wingate is an eighteen year-old American. He's the drummer. Julian can also play the trumpet, and you can hear his trumpet on three of the songs on the album.
Paul says about *Mickey can't dance: 'It's my favourite song from the album. We're all disabled in this group, but we can all see. There are many wonderful blind musicians, like Stevie Wonder and Ray Charles. The song is about a blind and disabled guitarist.'*

 **Mickey can't dance** (*Thomson-Raymond*)

Mickey can't walk,
and Mickey can't run,
and Mickey can't drive a car.
But Mickey can sing,
He can play the guitar,
He's a star . . . he's a star . . . he's a star.

Mickey can't see,
and Mickey can't read,
and Mickey can't do algebra.
But Mickey can sing,
He can play the guitar,
He's a star . . . he's a star . . . he's a star.

Mickey is blind, he can't see anything,
Mickey is blind, he can't read anything.
But Mickey is fine, he can sing anything,
Mickey is fine, he can play anything.

Mickey can't dance,
and Mickey can't swim.
No, Mickey can't go very far.
But Mickey can sing,
He can play the guitar,
He's a star . . . he's a star . . . he's a star.

a Meet Independence Day

Read about Independence Day in the *Music Mail.*

1 Complete this chart.

Name	Age	Nationality	Musical instruments
Paul Thomson			
Jill Raymond			
Denise Cooper			
Julian Wingate			

2 Work with another student. Ask and answer about the group.

A *Who's Paul Thomson?*
B *He's the guitarist and singer.*

A *Where's he from?*
B *He's from London.*

A *How old is he?*
B *He's 20.*

A *Which instruments can he play?*
B *He can play the guitar.*
He can play the piano. / He can also play the piano.

 Which languages can he speak?

Georges Schmidt is a translator at the United Nations. He's French. He can speak 30 languages. He can also translate from 36 other languages!
(from *The Guinness Book of Records*)
Which languages can he speak? Guess ten of the languages. Write sentences.

c Game: What can you do?

Look at these pictures. Ask other students the questions. Put a tick [✓] for *Yes, I can.*
Put a cross [✗] for *No, I can't.*
The winner is the first student with a tick in all the boxes.

1 Can you sing? 2 Can you speak three languages? 3 Can you type?

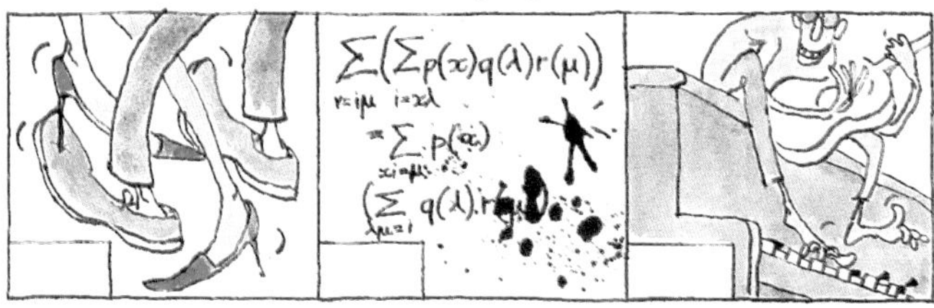

4 Can you dance? 5 Can you do algebra? 6 Can you play the guitar or the piano?

7 Can you swim 50 metres? 8 Can you/your father/your mother drive? 9 Can you write a postcard in English?

d What can they do?

Maria can play the saxophone. Peter can't dance.
Make sentences about other students in your class.

e A job interview

Read the advertisement and the letters.
Student A: Interview James (Student B) for the job.
Student B: Interview Tricia (Student A) for the job.

Wanted: **International Sales Representative**
for a multinational computer company.
The company has got offices in England, France, Japan, Spain, Holland, and Greece.

- Can you drive?
- Can you type?
- How many languages can you speak?
- Can you sell computers?

This is a wonderful job - for the right person.
Write to: Lemon Computers PLC
Bovis Street, Bradford, UK.

183 Belsize Road,
London,
NW6 2NJ

Dear Sir or Madam,
My name is James Hammond, and I'm 23 years old. I'm a salesman for a hi-fi company at the moment. I can speak French and Spanish. I've got a driving licence, and I can type. I don't know much about computers, but I can learn.

Personal details

Name	Tricia Miller
Address	17 Dalglish Avenue, Liverpool.
Age	25
Present job	Advertising Manager, 'Computer World' Magazine
Driving Licence	Yes
Typing	50 words per minute
Languages	French, Italian, German, Swedish

f Animal abilities

- A kangaroo can jump 13.5 metres.
- A blue whale can hear another blue whale 850 kilometres away.
- A cheetah can run at 100 km/h
- One type of swan (the whooper swan) can fly at 8,000 metres.
- A sperm whale can dive to one kilometre under the sea.
- A peregrine falcon can fly at 386 km/h (in a dive from 1,500 metres).

What time . . .?

ten o'clock

five past eight

ten past three

a quarter past six

THIS WEEK IN CASTERBRIDGE

Cinemas

Casterbridge 330225

CINEMA 1
Timothy Walton in
THE RETURN OF 007 (PG)
Doors open 2 p.m.
Performances:
2.25 / 4.35 / 6.25 / 8.35

CINEMA 2
Simon Stallion in
RUMBA 5 (18)
Doors open 2.15 p.m.
Performances:
2.40 / 4.20 / 6.40 / 8.20

CANNON CINEMAS
Casterbridge 330033

CANNON 1
Muriel Street / Ben Shawn in
THE FIRST TIME (15)
Performances daily at:
1.50 / 4.10 / 6.50 / 9.10

CANNON 2
New Children's Cartoon
THE MOUNTAIN OF GIANTS (U)
Children half price
Performances daily at:
1.55 / 3.05 / 4.55 / 6.05 / 7.55

Concerts and Ballet

★ THE ROYAL HALL, CASTERBRIDGE ★

Monday 8.30
CLASSICAL CONCERT
Charles Dubois & The Quebec Symphony Orchestra
HOLST: *The Planets*
RAVEL: *Bolero*
MAHLER: *5th Symphony*

Tuesday, Wednesday 9.15
ROCK CONCERT
Bruce Sprucetree
& The A-Road Band

Thursday, Friday, Saturday 7.45
BALLET
The Yorkshire Ballet in
Swan Lake

Sunday 7.30
JAZZ CONCERT
The David Miles Group
(David Miles, Rob Carter, Keith Jarrow, Bruce Billford)

Box Office: Casterbridge 220002

five to four

ten to five

a quarter to twelve

twenty to two

twenty past eleven

twenty-five past one

half past seven

twenty-five to nine

a This Week in Casterbridge

Look at This Week in Casterbridge, and answer these questions.

1 Which film is at five to two?
2 Which concert is at half past eight, the classical concert or the jazz concert?
3 What time is the rock concert?
4 What can you see on Thursday at The Royal Hall?
5 Which day can you go to a classical concert?
6 When is the first performance of *The Return of 007*?
7 When is the last performance of *The Mountain of Giants*?
8 Which film is Simon Stallion in?
9 What time is the first performance of *Rumba 5*?
10 What time is the next performance of *Rumba 5*?
11 Who is in *The Return of 007*?
12 What's the phone number of The Royal Hall?
13 Who can you see at The Royal Hall on Tuesday and Wednesday?
14 What time is *Swan Lake*?
15 When is the first performance of the Muriel Street film?
16 Where can you see a cartoon film?

b Cinemas

Look at Cinemas in This Week in Casterbridge.

A *Well, what would you like to see?*
B *What about (*Rumba 5*)?*
A *OK. When's the (next) performance?*
B *It's at (twenty to seven).*

the first / next / last performance

Make more conversations.

c Concerts and Ballet

Look at Concerts and Ballet in This Week in Casterbridge.

A *Can I have two tickets for (the Bruce Sprucetree concert), please?*
B *For which day?*
A *(Tuesday), please.*
B *Here you are.*
A *What time is (the concert)?*
B *It's at (a quarter past nine).*

Make more conversations.

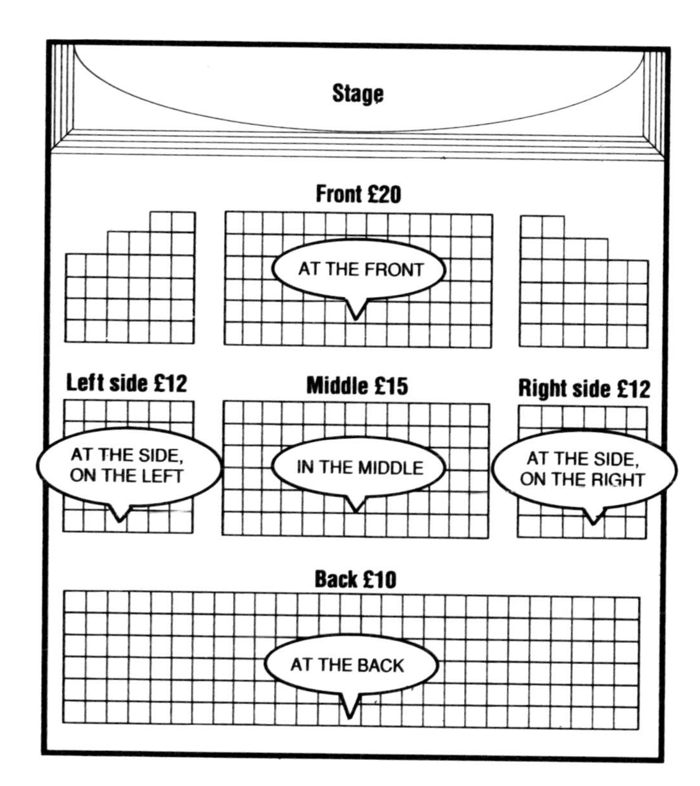

d The Royal Hall

Look at the plan of The Royal Hall.

A *Have you got any tickets for (Saturday)?*
B *Yes, we have. Where would you like to sit?*
A *Can we have two seats (at the back)?*
B *Yes, that's OK. Here you are . . . (W31 and W32).*
A *Thanks. How much is that?*
B *That's (£20).*
A *And what time is the performance?*
B *(A quarter to eight).*

Make more conversations.

e Three conversations

Listen to these three conversations.
Put a tick [✓] by the correct answer.

1 a How much are the tickets altogether?
☐ £4 ☐ £14 ☐ £40
b What time's the next performance?
☐ 5.20 ☐ 5.40 ☐ 4.40

2 a The tickets are for . . .
☐ today ☐ Thursday ☐ Tuesday
b They'd like seats . . .
☐ in the middle ☐ at the side ☐ at the front
c The Royal Hall has got seats free . . .
☐ at the front ☐ on the right ☐ in the middle

3 a The first performance is at . . .
☐ 2.05 ☐ 1.55 ☐ 2.55
b The next performance is at . . .
☐ 3.55 ☐ 3.05 ☐ 2.55
c How much are the tickets each?
☐ £3.15 ☐ £350 ☐ £3.50

Flight 201

Pilot Good evening, ladies and gentlemen. My name's Captain Yeager, and this is Flight 201 to Rome. We're flying over Paris at the moment. Our flight attendants are serving dinner and drinks. Have a good flight . . . Thank you.

Gina Here's your coffee, Captain.
Pilot Thanks, Gina. Is everything OK?
Gina Oh, yes, sir. The passengers have got their dinners. They're all eating and drinking.
Pilot Good. What's that noise?
Gina I don't know . . .
Pilot Go and look.
Gina Oh! It's an old lady at the front of the plane!
Pilot What's she doing?
Gina Er . . . she's hitting the window, sir . . . with her shoe . . .
Pilot What! Go and stop her!

Gina Excuse me, madam. What are you doing?
Lady It's very hot in here, and I can't open this window. Can you help me, Miss?
Pilot What's wrong, Gina?
Lady Who are you?
Pilot I'm the pilot, madam.
Lady Oh no! Who's flying the plane?
Pilot It's all right, madam. There are two pilots, and it's . . .
Co-pilot Is everything all right?
Lady Who's he?
Co-pilot I'm the co-pilot, madam . . .
Lady But you aren't flying the plane!
Co-pilot No, madam. It's got an automatic pilot!

a What are they doing?

Look at the picture of the plane.

There's an old lady at the front.
A *What's she doing?*
B *She's hitting the window.*

1 There's a man behind her.
2 There are two women behind him.
3 There's a man behind them.
4 There's a man on the right.
5 There's a woman behind him.
6 There are two people behind her.

Make questions and answers.
Use these words: *stand / drink / listen to / read / sleep / eat.*

do - doing

do - doing	sit - sitting
drink - drinking	eat - eating
speak - speaking	fly - flying
hit - hitting	wear - wearing
stand - standing	serve - serving
sleep - sleeping	read - reading
look - looking	listen - listening

b Yes, he is./No, he isn't.

Look at **a What are they doing?**

There's a man behind the old lady.
A *Is he eating?*
B *No, he isn't.*
A *Is he sleeping?*
B *No, he isn't.*
A *Is he reading?*
B *Yes, he is.*
A *Is he reading a book?*
B *No, he isn't reading a book.*
A *What is he reading?*
B *He's reading a magazine.*

Ask and answer about the other people on the plane.

c Traffic jam

What are these people doing? Ask and answer.

Comet!

Patrick Good evening. It's midnight, and this is 'World Report' from London. My name's Patrick Shaw. Tonight we're talking about the new comet. People can see it in sixty countries. The huge new comet is travelling through space. It's coming towards the Earth, and it's very near us now. We've got reports from three places.

1 The Sahara Desert

Patrick Our reporter, Jan Lenton, is in the Sahara Desert. Hello Jan. What's happening?

Jan Hello, Patrick. It's one o'clock in the morning here. I'm standing on a hill in the desert. The sky is very clear, and I can see the comet. It's moving across the sky. It's huge and it's very bright. We aren't using television lights, but you can see me. It's amazing!

2 Antarctica

Patrick Mike Worsley is in Antarctica. Hello, Mike. What's happening there? Can you hear me?

Mike Yes, Patrick. We can hear you. Well, we're driving across the ice, and the comet is high in the sky. We can see everything. We're near the sea, but there aren't any penguins on the ice here. They're all swimming in the sea. They're afraid of the comet, I think.

3 New York

Patrick Our last report is from New York City. Hello, New York. What's happening?

Karen Hello, London. This is Karen Buckley from NBC News in New York. It's seven o'clock in the evening here, and there are thousands of people on the streets. They're watching the sky. We can see the comet, and it's fantastic! Some people are taking photographs, some people are singing and dancing in the streets. But many people are afraid. There are thousands of birds in the sky. They're flying away from the city.

Athens is two hours ahead of London.

Brazil is four hours behind London.

New York, USA. 6 a.m. January 10th

Rio de Janeiro, Brazil. 7 a.m. January 10th

London, England. 11 a.m. January 10th

Nairobi, Kenya. 2 p.m. January 10th

Tokyo, Japan. 8 p.m. January 10th

Sydney, Australia. 10 p.m. January 10th

a What are they doing?

Look at the pictures.
Where is it? What time is it? What are they doing?
Ask and answer.

b When it's 6 a.m. in New York . . .

When it's 6 a.m. in New York, it's 2 p.m. in Nairobi.
1 Make sentences like this about the pictures.
2 Make sentences about other towns.

c When they're having breakfast in Rio . . .

When they're having breakfast in Rio, they're having dinner in Japan.
1 Make sentences like this about the pictures.
2 Make sentences about other towns.

d Months

January	April	July	October
February	May	August	November
March	June	September	December

December is the twelfth month.
1 Make sentences about all the months.

What is the eleventh month?
2 Ask and answer eleven questions like this.

e What are they doing now?

A *What's your mother doing now?*
B *My mother's driving to work. / I think my mother's driving to work.*
A *What are your friends doing now?*
B *My friends are playing tennis. / I think my friends are playing tennis.*
Ask and answer about your family and friends.

K Division Metro Police

Inside

Cobb Well, are you going to take any photographs, or not? Hey, Kennedy! I'm talking to you!
Kennedy Oh, sorry, Sarge. No, it's very quiet. Nothing's happening.
Cobb I'm going to have a sleep. Don't wake me, all right?
Kennedy OK, Sarge.
Voice Hello, Mr Hooper? Are you there? Mr Hooper? It's me, Mrs Harris. Are you all right?

Lady Who are you? What are you doing here? Where's Mr Hooper?
Cobb Er, Mr Hooper isn't here, I'm a friend . . .
Lady I'm going to phone the police . . .
Cobb We *are* the police. Look at this, love. Detective Sergeant Cobb, K Division, Metro Police. This is Detective Kennedy. It's all right.
Lady But what are you doing here? What's happening?
Cobb It's police business, love. Don't tell anybody, OK?
Lady Ooh! It's very exciting! I'm Mrs Harris from downstairs. Would you like a cup of tea?
Cobb No, thanks. Goodbye.
Lady Goodbye.
Kennedy She's a nice old lady.
Cobb Yeah. What's happening outside?
Kennedy Nothing. Wait a minute! A car's coming along the street.
Cobb The camera . . . quick!

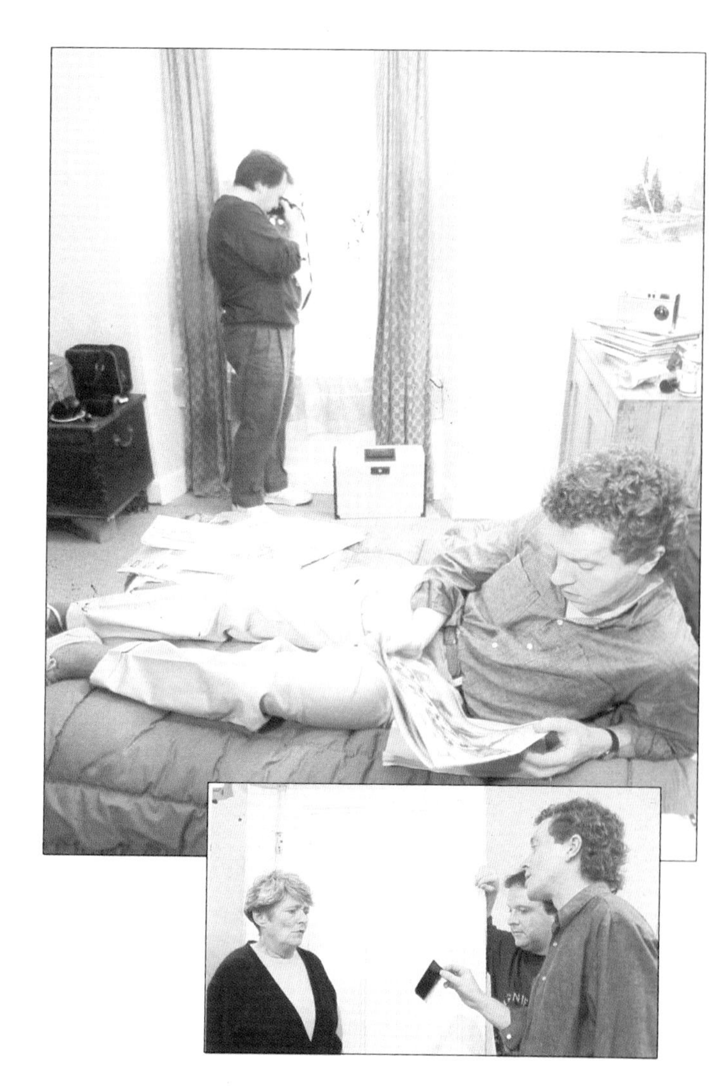

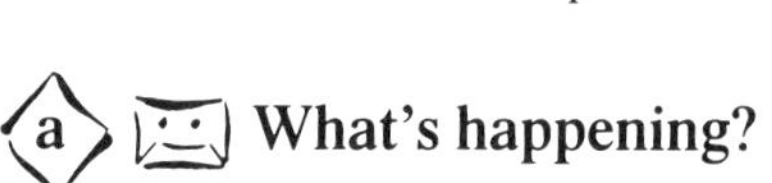

a What's happening?

Look at the pictures. Listen to the next part of the story.

Outside

Cobb Come on, Kennedy . . . start the engine . . . hurry! Tango Delta to Control. Come to the High Street. There's going to be a robbery . . .

Cobb Where are they? They aren't in the bank . . .
Kennedy Have they got guns, Sarge?
Cobb I don't know. Why?
Kennedy Well . . . we haven't!
Cobb Look! They're over there.

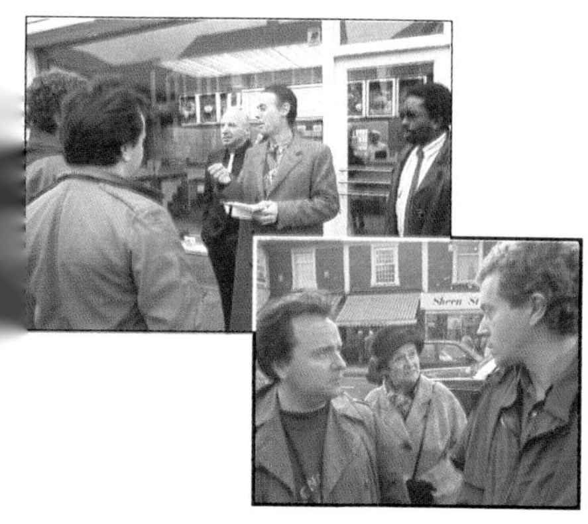

Craig Hello! It's Sergeant Cobb. How are you today, Sergeant?
Cobb What are you doing, Craig?
Craig I'm having my lunch, Sergeant. Would you like a chip? Oh, and Sergeant Cobb, these are my friends, Mr Bailey and Mr Daniels.
Daniels Pleased to meet you, Sergeant.
Craig Oh, and I'd like you to meet my mother.
Cobb Your mother?
Craig Yes, she's behind you.
Lady How do you do, Sergeant? It's nice to see you . . . again.

(b) What are they going to do?

Look at picture 1.
A *Is he taking a photograph?*
B *No, he isn't.*

A *Is he going to take a photograph?*
B *Yes, he is.*

A *What's he going to do?*
B *He's going to take a photograph.*

Look at picture 2.
A *What's he doing?*
B *He's taking a photograph.*

Make sentences about the pictures.

The secret of the pyramid

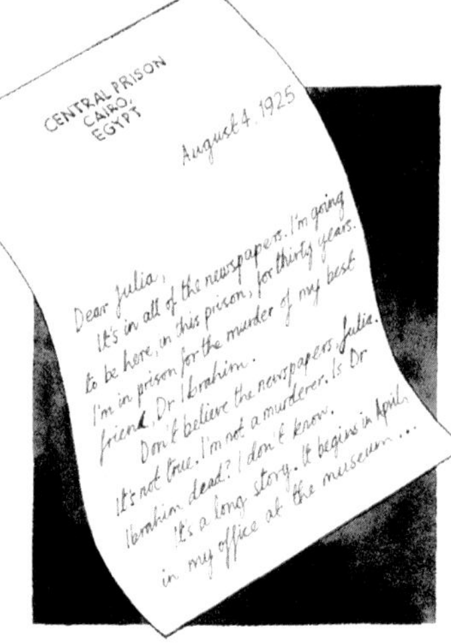

CENTRAL PRISON
CAIRO,
EGYPT

August 4, 1925

Dear Julia,

It's in all of the newspapers. I'm going to be here, in this prison, for thirty years. I'm in prison for the murder of my best friend, Dr Ibrahim.

Don't believe the newspapers Julia. It's not true. I'm not a murderer. Is Dr Ibrahim dead? I don't know.

It's a long story. It begins in April, in my office at the museum ...

THAT'S IT! THE DOOR'S OPEN. FOLLOW ME...

AARGH! WHAT'S THAT!

IT'S A SKELETON... FROM ONE OF THE WORKERS ON THE PYRAMID. IT'S ABOUT 4,000 YEARS OLD! WELL, WE KNOW SOMETHING... KAMUN IV'S SECRET IS A VERY IMPORTANT ONE. LOOK THERE'S A KNIFE IN THE SKELETON.

HERE'S ANOTHER DOOR. CAN YOU READ THE WRITING?
IT'S ANOTHER CURSE, THIS IS THE HOUSE OF THE DEAD. OPEN THE DOOR... AND DIE!

WELL, I'M GOING TO OPEN IT...
WAIT! DON'T WALK IN! PUSH THE DOOR OPEN WITH THIS...

SEE, THERE'S A KNIFE BEHIND THE DOOR!
TWANG
THANK YOU DR IBRAHIM. WE CAN GO IN NOW.

WE'RE THE FIRST PEOPLE IN THIS ROOM FOR 4,000 YEARS! LOOK. THERE'S GOLD!

AND A COFFIN! IT'S NOT HEAVY, WE CAN OPEN IT. BUT BE VERY CAREFUL...

IT'S A MUMMY... BUT IS IT KAMUN IV?

BANG!
WHAT'S THAT!
THE DOOR. IT'S CLOSED. HAVE YOU GOT ANY MATCHES?

YES, IT'S ALL RIGHT. HERE'S THE LIGHT. OH NO! THE COFFIN'S EMPTY. THE MUMMY ISN'T THERE. WHERE IS IT? AND WHAT ARE WE GOING TO DO NOW?

AH, THE MUMMY'S HERE, ON THE GROUND. IBRAHIM? IBRAHIM? WHERE ARE YOU?

Outside the Pyramid.
WHERE'S DR IBRAHIM?
I DON'T KNOW...
Well, Julia, the police don't believe my story. The workers don't believe me. Maybe you don't believe me. The police say I'm a murderer... a murderer for the gold in the pyramid.
The gold is with the coffin in the museum now. But that isn't the secret of the pyramid. Maybe Dr Ibrahim knows the secret now. But where is he?
Write to me, please.
Your brother,
Wilfred
Wilfred Dean. Prisoner number 671825.

The weather

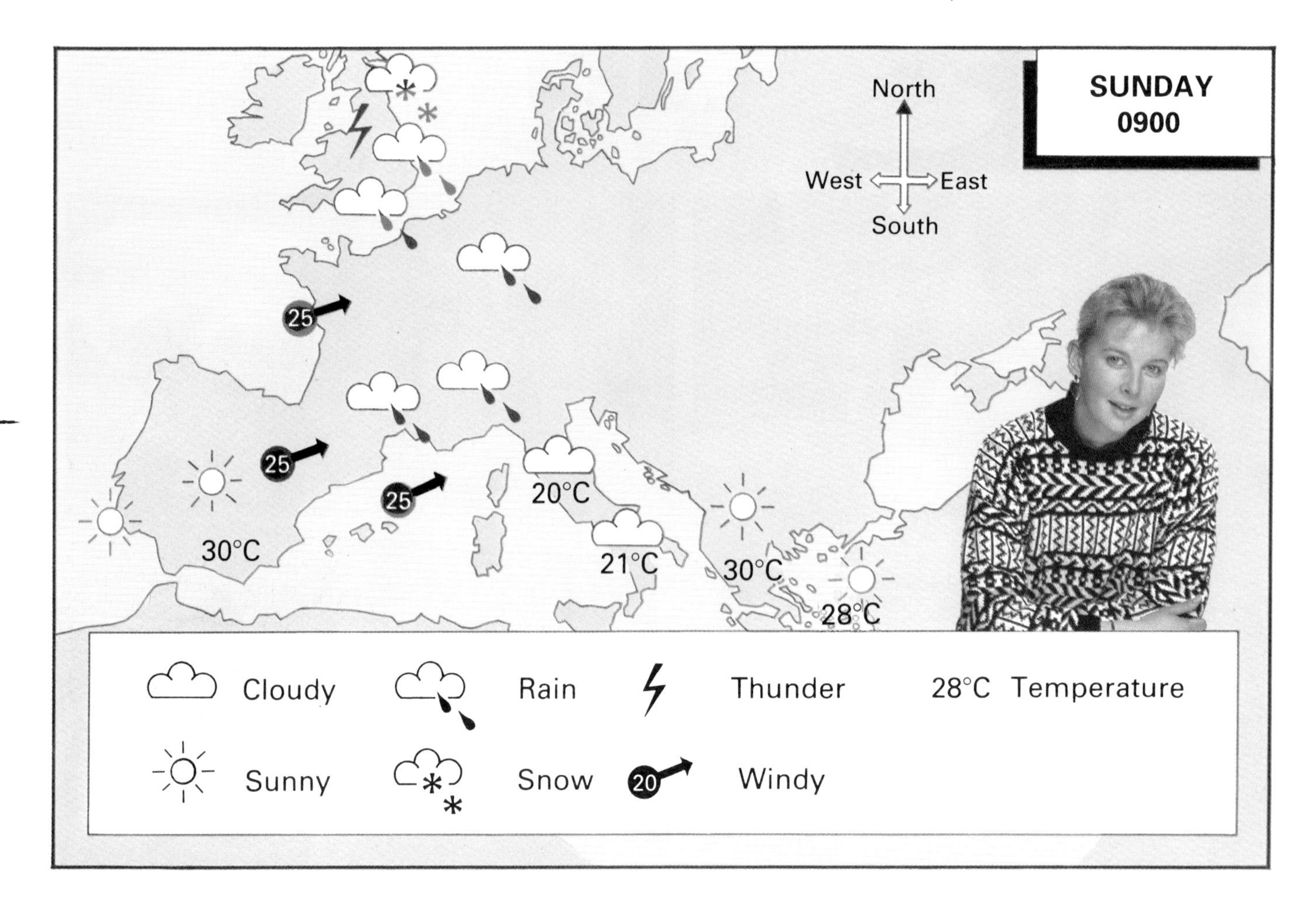

Good evening. This is Gale Fawcett with the weather forecast for tomorrow. It's Easter Saturday, and a lot of people are going away on holiday. We're going to look at the European weather map for tomorrow morning at 9 o'clock.

First, the bad news. It's raining in Spain at the moment. And the good news? It isn't going to rain tomorrow! It's going to be a hot, sunny day, with temperatures of 30 degrees Celsius.

The rain is going to move into France tonight. Tomorrow is going to be wet and windy in the South of France. In Italy it's going to be a dry day, but cloudy. The temperature there is going to be about 20 or 21 degrees Celsius.

What about Greece? Well, the sun's going to shine there. A very hot day, with temperatures about 30 degrees in Athens, 27 or 28 degrees in the islands.

And Britain? Sorry, but it's going to be a cold, wet day again. It's going to snow in Scotland, and there's going to be thunder in the North of England. Have a nice holiday!

going to future

It	's isn't	going to be	hot / cold. dry / wet. sunny / cloudy. warm / cool.

It	's isn't	going to	rain. snow. thunder.

There's	going to be	rain. snow. thunder.

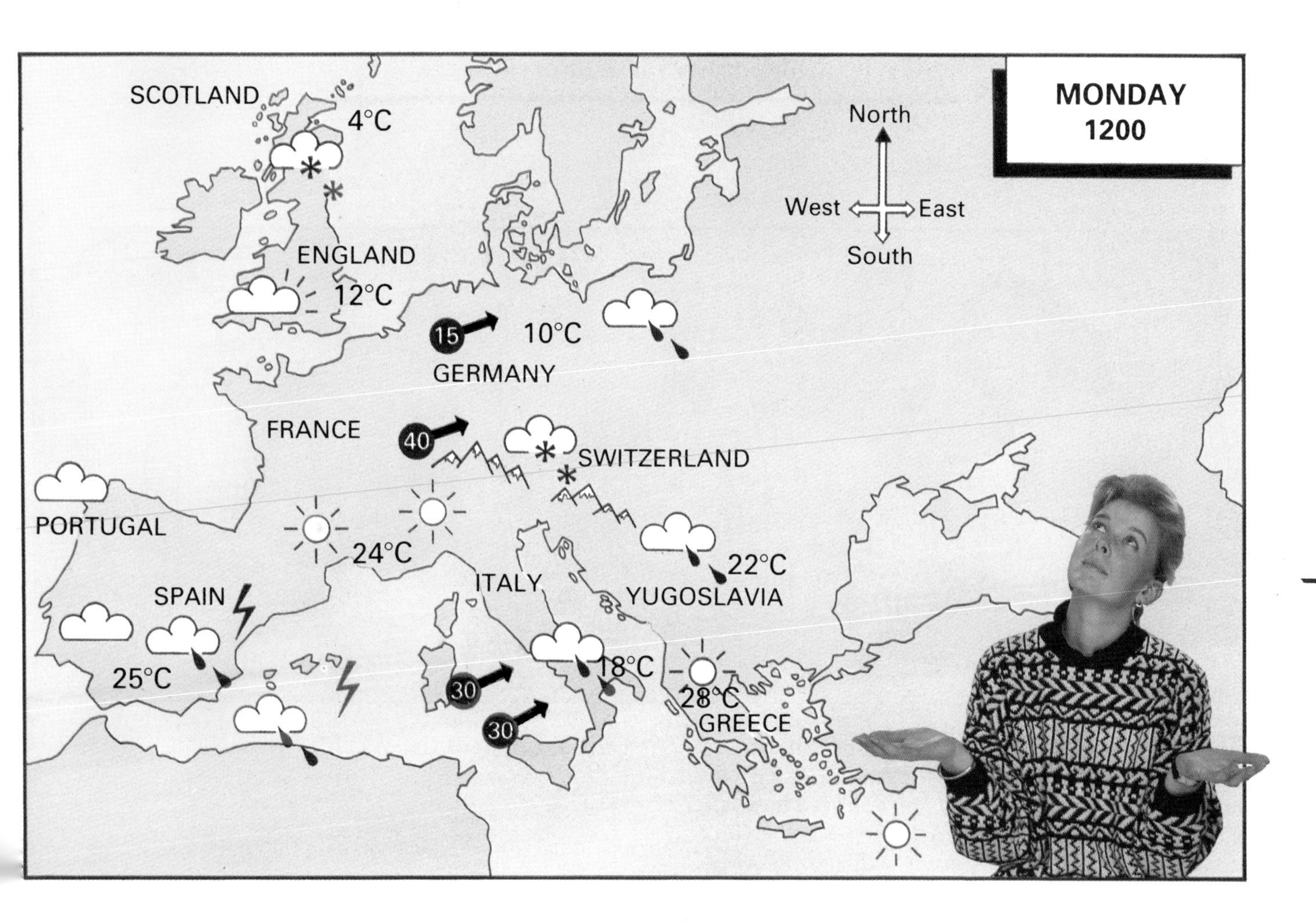

a Monday's weather

1 Look at the weather map for Monday at 12 o'clock.
What's the weather going to be like in:
France / Spain / Portugal / England / Italy / Scotland / Greece / Yugoslavia / Germany?
Ask and answer.

2 Write a weather forecast for one country.

b Your country

What's the weather like today?

What's the weather going to be like | *tomorrow?* / *next week?* / *next month?* / *next summer?* / *next winter?*

Ask and answer.

c What are you going to do?

What are you going to do | *this morning?* / *this afternoon?* / *this evening?* / *tonight?* / *tomorrow?*

Make sentences.

d Questionnaire

Are you going to:

- ☐ *stay at home?*
- ☐ *watch TV?*
- ☐ *listen to music?*
- ☐ *go out?*
- ☐ *meet someone?*

Ask three students.
Put ticks [✓] for yes, and crosses [✗] for no, then ask:

***Which** programmes are you going to watch?*
***What** are you going to listen to?*
***Where** are you going to go?*
***When** are you going to go there?*
***What time** are you going to come home?*
***How much** money are you going to spend?*
***How many** people are you going to meet / talk to?*
***Who** are you going to meet / talk to?*

She doesn't like interviews

Lisa is a reporter for *Fortnight* magazine. She's interviewing Suzanne Jacklin, the American writer. Suzanne is the author of *Kiss*. The book is a best seller in ten languages, and there is a TV series and a film, too. Her agent, Frank DeVito, is with her.

Lisa Ms Jacklin, is this your first visit to England?
Suzanne Well, er . . . no . . .
Frank No, it isn't. Next question.
Lisa Do you like England?
Suzanne Well, yes, I do . . .
Frank Yes, she does. Next question.
Lisa Do you like English men?
Suzanne Well, er, I . . .
Frank No, she doesn't. No way!
Lisa Ms Jacklin, I like the book *Kiss*, but I don't like the film. Do you like the film?
Suzanne Well, I . . .
Frank She likes it very much. It's a wonderful film, a box office success . . . twenty million dollars in the first week!
Lisa I'm asking her, Mr DeVito.
Frank She doesn't like interviews. I'm answering the questions, OK?
Lisa OK. Does she like the television series of *Kiss*?
Frank Yes, she li . . .
Suzanne DeVito . . .
Frank Yes, Ms Jacklin?
Suzanne Shut up. No, I don't. I don't like the television series, and I don't like the film. That's the end of the interview. Goodbye.

Woman of the Week

WOMAN OF THE WEEK

Suzanne Jacklin

Suzanne is the author of
Love in L.A., King, Star, and Kiss

AGE *37*
★
NATIONALITY *American*
★
FAVOURITE COLOUR *Pink*
★
FAVOURITE SPORT *Swimming*
★
FAVOURITE FOOD *Salad*
★
FAVOURITE DRINK *Champagne*
★
LIKES
Old Hollywood films, shopping, reading, cats
★
DISLIKES
New Hollywood films, classical music, dogs, meat

This is from *Fortnight* magazine.

Make sentences with: *She likes . . . / She doesn't like . . .*

Role play

Look at Woman of the Week.
Student A (Lisa): interview Student B (Suzanne Jackli

c Likes and dislikes

SPORTS

FOOD

MUSIC

CLOTHES

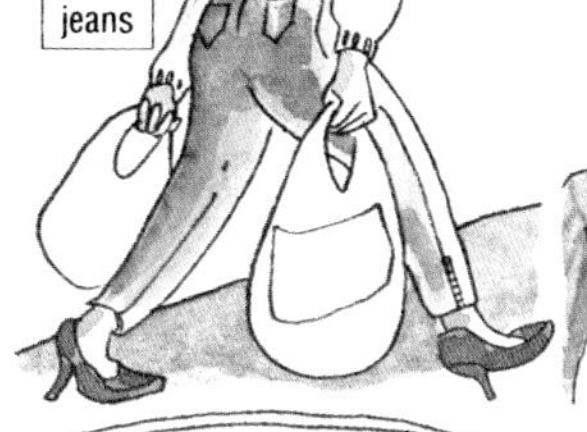

T V

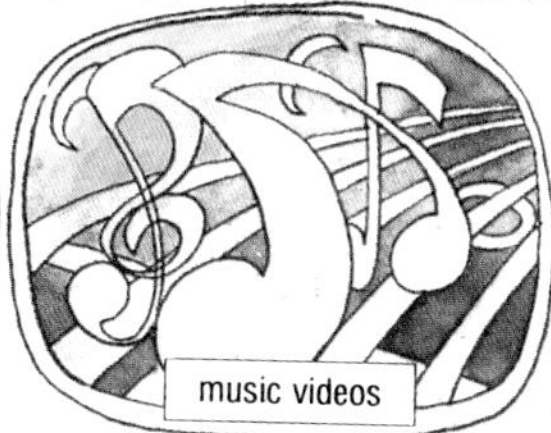

1 Ask another student questions.

A *Do you like football?*
B *Yes, I do. / No, I don't.*

Put a tick [✓] for yes, and a cross [✗] for no.

2 Work with a different student.

A *Does she like football?*
B *Yes, she does. / No, she doesn't.*

Talk about the answers in **1** above.

3 Work with the same student.

A *Which sports do you like?*
B *I like football and tennis. I don't like swimming.*

Ask and answer.

4 Work with a different student.

A *Which sports does he like?*
B *He likes football and tennis. He doesn't like swimming.*

Talk about the answers in **3** above.

d The ABC of likes

	likes	dislikes
A	apples, Prince Andrew	American food, algebra
B	BMW cars, bikes, blue	brown clothes, Beethoven
C	Christmas, the country	cities, computers, cats
D	______________	______________

1 Write a list from A to Z.
(Don't worry about X and Z!)

2 Ask another student about his/her list, and talk about your list.

Wants and needs

a Chris's room

Match things in the picture with the words below.

1 bookcase	**9** clock
2 cupboard	**10** tennis racket
3 waste bin	**11** mirror
4 desk	**12** carpet
5 light	**13** curtains
6 poster	**14** wardrobe
7 shelf	**15** suitcase
8 plant	**16** bed

Chris is going to college next week. He's tidying his room at home, and his sister, Sally, is helping him. Chris is throwing some things away. He doesn't want them any more, but Sally would like some of his things.

Sally Chris, do you want this poster?
Chris Which one?
Sally This one. The Michael Jackson poster. Do you want it?
Chris No. Put it in the waste bin.
Sally Don't you like Michael Jackson any more?
Chris Oh, yes. I like his music. But I don't want the poster.
Sally Hmm. It's a nice picture.
Chris Would you like it?
Sally OK. Thanks.

Sally What about this plant.
Chris The cactus? No, you can have it.
Sally I don't want it. I don't like it. Anyway, it's dead.
Chris Throw it away, then. Do you want these magazines?
Sally No, thanks.

Sally You've got two bins. Do you need them?
Chris Well . . .
Sally You only need one. Can I have the blue one?
Chris Yes, all right. I don't need it.

Sally What are these?
Chris Where?
Sally Here. On the bookcase.
Chris Oh, they're my diplomas.
Sally Do you want them? They're very old.
Chris Yes, I do!
Sally Why?
Chris Because . . . because . . . Oh, I don't know! I just want them, that's all.

b Your room

1 Think about your room. Write lists.

(I've got and) I like . . .	(I've got and) I don't like . . .	(I've got and) I don't need . . .	(I haven't got and) I want . . .
1			
2			
3			

2 Ask another student:
What have you got?
What do you like?
What don't you like?
What don't you need?
What do you want?

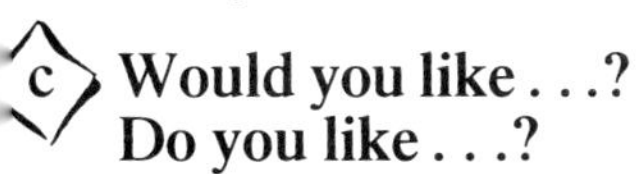

c Would you like . . .? Do you like . . .?

A *Would you like some fish 'n' chips?*
B *No, thanks.*
A *Oh? Don't you like fish 'n' chips?*
B *Yes, I do. But I don't want any now. I'm not hungry.*

Do you like Pepsi-Cola?
Yes, I do.
Would you like some now?
No, thanks. I'm not thirsty.

lake conversations with these
ords: a hot dog / a hamburger /
epsi-Cola / chips / coffee /
hocolate biscuits / hungry / thirsty.

HOUSESTORES PLC STORE GUIDE

Lower Ground Floor	Kitchen equipment ◆ Coffee shop ◆ Hardware ◆ Lighting ◆ Electrical goods ◆ Florist ◆ House plants ◆
Ground Floor	Cosmetics ◆ Stationery ◆ Bookshop ◆ Pharmacy ◆ Confectionery ◆
First Floor	Ladies' fashions ◆ Ladies' shoes ◆ Girls' fashions ◆ Children's clothes ◆ Children's shoes ◆ Babies' clothes ◆ Toys ◆
Second Floor	Sports equipment ◆ Sports clothes ◆ Radio & television ◆ Hi-Fi ◆ Record department ◆ Men's clothes ◆ Men's shoes ◆
Third floor	Furniture ◆ Curtains ◆ Soft furnishings ◆ Fabrics ◆ Bed linen ◆
Fourth floor	Roof-top restaurant ◆ Hairdresser ◆ Toilets ◆ Accounts department ◆

d Which floor?

Look at the people in the lift. Which floors do they want?

1 __ 2 __ 3 __ 4 __ 5 __ 6 __ 7 __ 8 __ 9 __ 10 __

e Needs

Plants need sunlight, water, earth.
Complete these sentences:
People need . . . *Cars need . . .* *Cities need . . .*
Schools need . . . *Children need . . .* *The world needs . . .*

Regular hours?

DO YOU WORK REGULAR HOURS?

There are two kinds of job. Some people work 'regular hours'. In England they work from nine to five, or nine to five thirty every day. In other countries they work in the mornings from eight to one, and in the evenings from five to nine every day. But they always work at the same times every day, for five or six days a week. These are 'regular hours'.

Some people don't work at the same times every day, and they don't work on the same days every week. They work 'irregular hours'. Their lives are very different. They don't see their families every day. They don't get the same money every week.

Here are some examples.

REGULAR HOURS

Tracy lives in London. She works in an office. She begins work at nine every day. She has lunch from twelve thirty to one thirty, and she finishes work at five. She goes out with her friends in the evenings.

Tracy Crabtree

Gurnam lives in Manchester. He works in a factory. He always begins work at eight, and finishes at four thirty. He always works five days a week. He never works on Saturdays and Sundays. He's married, and he's got three children. He sees his family in the evenings every day.

Gurnam Singh

Carmen lives in Spain. She works in a shop. She always begins work at nine o'clock, and works until one thirty. Then she goes home for lunch with her family. She begins work again at five, and works until eight or nine in the evening. She never works on Sundays and Mondays.

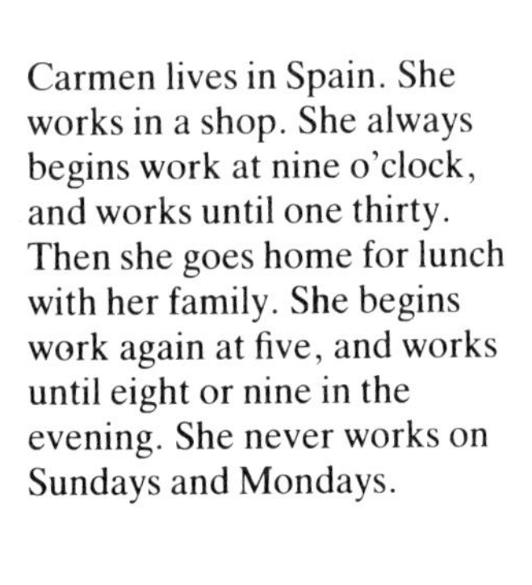

Carmen García

IRREGULAR HOURS

Colin Shelton

Colin works on an oil rig in the North Sea. He works ten hours a day, seven days a week for two weeks. He lives on the oil rig, and sometimes he works twelve or fifteen hours a day. Then he goes home for ten days. Colin lives in Leeds.

Shelley O'Connell

Shelley is a flight attendant. She lives in Dublin in Ireland, and works for Aer Lingus, the Irish airline. She doesn't come home every night. Sometimes she stays in hotels in European cities. She works for four or five days. Then she has three or four days off.

George Samson

George is a famous writer. He lives in New York, and writes detective stories. He writes two books every year. He goes to a hotel, and works eighteen hours a day, seven days a week, for three weeks. He doesn't see anybody. He finishes a book in three weeks. Then he doesn't write for six months.

a Whose job?

Look at the jobs on the left.
Whose job would you like? Why?
Which kind of job would you like? A job with regular hours or a job with irregular hours? Why?

b Shift work

Some people work shifts, e.g. police officers, nurses, taxi drivers.
Nurses work in three shifts:
Early shift 6 a.m. – 2 p.m.
Late shift 2 p.m. – 10 p.m.
Night shift 10 p.m. – 6 a.m.
Would you like shift work? Why? / Why not?

c Four jobs

You are going to hear four people. They are talking about their jobs.
Listen and complete the chart.
S M T W T F S = Sunday
Monday
Tuesday
Wednesday
Thursday
Friday
Saturday

e Questions

Ask and answer.

1 What time do you begin work?
2 Do you always finish at the same time?
3 How many hours do you work every day?
4 How many days do you work every week?

Think about someone you know. (Your father, mother, a friend.)

5 What time does he/she begin work?
6 What time does he/she finish?
7 How many hours does he/she work every day?
8 How many days does he/she work every week?

f Game: Think of a job

Every student thinks of a job. One student comes to the front of the class. The class can ask ten questions. The student at the front can answer Yes or No.

1 A *Do you work inside?*
B *Yes, I do.*
2 A *Do you work in an office?*
B *No, I don't.*
3 A *Do you always start work at the same time?*
B *No, I don't.*
4 . . .

Can you guess the job in ten questions?

Job	Starting time	Workdays tick [✓]	Work on Sundays? tick [✓]	Are they regular hours? [yes/no]
1		S M T W T F S	always sometimes never	
2		S M T W T F S	always sometimes never	
3		S M T W T F S	always sometimes never	
4		S M T W T F S	always sometimes never	

d Regular hours?

Do these people work regular hours?
Talk to another student.

a president
a rock singer
a film director
a pilot
a waiter
a nurse
a teacher
a writer
a taxi driver
an actor
a secretary
a boxer
a doctor
a reporter
a priest

A day in the life of Dennis Cook

Dennis Cook lives at 23 Primrose Avenue.

Dennis is 37. He's married. His wife, Tricia, is 34.

Dennis usually wakes up at seven o'clock.

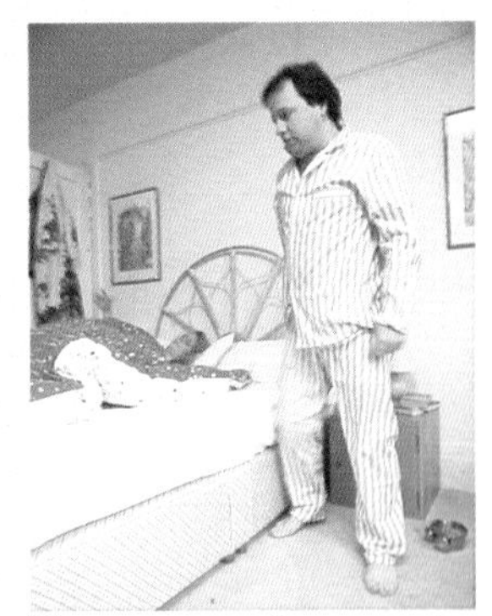

He gets up and goes to the bathroom.

Dennis cleans his teeth, and he shaves.

Then he has a shower.

He goes back to the bedroom, and he puts on his clothes.

Then he goes downstairs, and goes into the kitchen.

He makes a cup of tea.

Then he takes a cup of tea upstairs to Tricia.

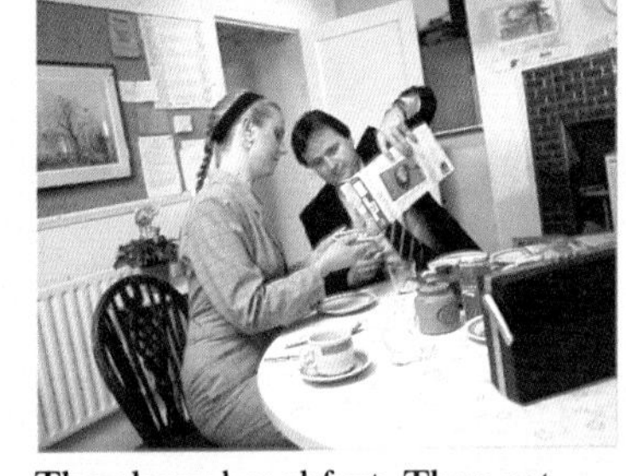

They have breakfast. They eat cornflakes, and drink orange juice.

Dennis reads *The Times*, and Trici listens to the radio.

Dennis leaves the house at 8.15.

He always kisses Tricia.

Then he drives to work.

He gets out of his car, and goes to work.

He opens his case. He plays his guitar.

He usually has lunch at 12.30.

In the afternoon, he plays the guitar again.

He usually stops work at five o'clock.

He comes home at half past five, and kisses Tricia.

They usually have dinner at seven o'clock.

In the evening, they watch television.

And here is the nine o'clock news . .

They usually go to bed at eleven o'clock. That's another exciting day in the life of . . . Dennis Cook.

a Dennis Cook's day

What time does he usually wake up?
What does he do then?
When does he have lunch?
What does he do at work?
What do Dennis and Tricia do in the evening?

Ask another student about Dennis Cook's day.

b Your day

What time do you usually wake up?
What do you do then?
When do you have lunch?
What do you do in the evening?

1 Ask another student about his/her day.
2 Tell him/her about your day.

c Tricia Cook's day

7.00 wake up
7.45 have breakfast
8.45 leave home
9.30 begin work
(Tricia is a dentist)
1.00 have lunch
4.45 finish work
5.00 drive home
7.00 have dinner
7.45 watch television
11.00 go to bed

Ask another student about Tricia Cook's day.

d My day

Write about your day.

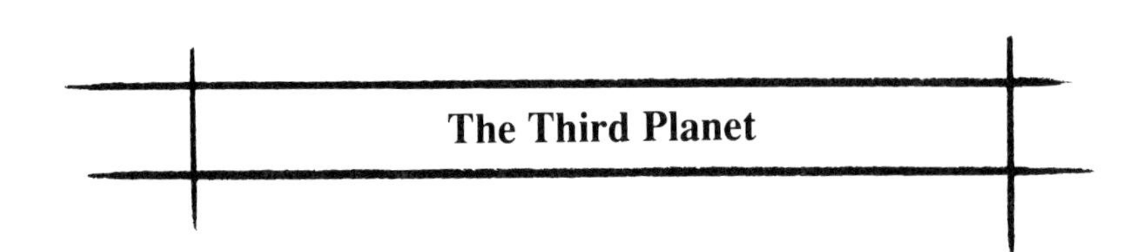

The Third Planet

To: Galaxy Central Command, Planet Volkan.
From: Spaceship 40956148
Subject: Solar System, The Third Planet. Report 1.

Spaceship 40956148 is now above the Third Planet in the Solar System. The planet has an area of 510,165,600 square kms. 71% of this is water. There are three types of intelligent life on the planet: 1) *dolphins* 2) *whales* 3) *humans*. Types 1 and 2 are very intelligent, but they live in water. Our people can't live in water. We are going to look at type 3, the humans. My assistant, Space Technician Bizaldo, likes the planet. This is strange. The planet is not beautiful. It is blue and green. I am thinking about my beautiful home on the planet Glom, with its red sky!

Space Commander Zook

To: Galaxy Central Command, Planet Volkan.
From: Spaceship 40956148
Subject: The Third Planet. Report 2. The humans.

The humans are very much like us. They have got two legs, two arms, two eyes etc. But they have only got ten fingers (five on each hand), and they haven't got green hair. They work about eight hours a day. On Glom we work twenty hours a day! (Their day is twenty-four hours, our day is twenty-two hours.) They eat three or four times a day, and sleep for six or eight hours a day. Space Technician Bizaldo thinks they are wonderful. Bizaldo likes eating and sleeping. He sometimes sleeps two or even three hours a day! I am very angry with Bizaldo. Now he wants food three or four times a day, like the humans! Well, he can't have food three times a day. He's a Glommite like me, and we only need one meal a week.

Space Commander Zook

To: Galaxy Central Command, Planet Volkan.
From: Spaceship 40956148
Subject: The Third Planet. Report 3. The humans.

We are now above an island in the north of the Third Planet. There are many different animals on the planet. On this island there is a very important animal, the *dog*. It has got four legs. It lives in houses with the humans! Every day the dogs take the humans out of the houses for a walk. The dogs have got ropes round them, and they pull the humans behind them. The dogs stop and smell trees, and the humans stop too. I think the humans work for the dogs. Space Technician Bizaldo doesn't think I am correct, but he is crazy. The journey home from the Third Planet is only fifteen years in a Glommite spaceship, but Space Technician Bizaldo cannot wait. He wants to go down and walk on the Third Planet! I say, 'Bizaldo, don't be silly! In fifteen more years you can walk on the beautiful orange ground on Glom.' Bizaldo wants to eat food from the Third Planet, too!

Space Commander Zook

To: Galaxy Central Command, Planet Volkan.
From: Spaceship 40956148
Subject: The Third Planet. Report 4. The humans.

I am worried about Space Technician Bizaldo. He watches television programmes from the Third Planet all the time. He thinks they are *funny.* He is watching a television programme now, and he is *laughing*. We never laugh on Glom. His favourite programmes are about two animals, *Mickey Mouse* and *Donald Duck*. In the programmes the mouse and the duck can talk, and they wear clothes. This is silly. There are animals like this on the Third Planet, but they can't talk and they don't wear clothes. I don't understand the programmes. But I don't understand Space Technician Bizaldo. We are recording radio and television programmes from Planet Three. The music is terrible, but Space Technician Bizaldo likes it. He sometimes sings with the music. It is a terrible noise. I have got a headache.

Space Commander Zook

To: Galaxy Central Command, Planet Volkan.
From: Spaceship 40956148
Subject: The Third Planet. Report 5. The humans.

Our spaceship is over another area of the Third Planet. The human name for this area is *California*. Today we are looking at some more humans. They are on a beach near a very big area of water. The humans call it *The Pacific Ocean.* They are sitting on the beach, and they aren't wearing many clothes. They are sitting in the sun. I think this is very silly. We all know about radioactivity from suns. The temperature on the beach is about 30°C. I am thinking about my beautiful Glom, the temperature there is always about 2°C. We have wonderful cold rain all the time, and sometimes on nice days we have fog! Space Technician Bizaldo wants to go down to the beach. He says it is lovely down there! He sings human music all the time now.

Space Commander Zook

To: Galaxy Central Command, Planet Volkan.
From: Spaceship 40956148
Subject: The Third Planet. Report 6. The humans.

Space Technician Bizaldo is very excited today. We are above California again. We are over a big sports stadium. There are about 100,000 humans down there. Bizaldo is listening to a radio programme. He says the big meeting is a *rock concert.* The noise is very bad. We can see the musicians. Some of them have got green hair like us. (Some have pink hair and orange hair too. This is strange. Humans usually do not have green or pink or orange hair.) I am going to work on the spaceship's engines today. Bizaldo wants to listen to the music, and my headache is terrible. I can't stay in the control room with him.

Space Commander Zook

To: Galaxy Central Command, Planet Volkan.
From: Spaceship 40956148
Subject: Space Technician Bizaldo.

I have got very bad news. Space Technician Bizaldo isn't on the spaceship. I am sorry, very sorry. He is on the Third Planet. I can see him on the television screen. He is with the musicians, the ones with green hair. He wants to stay there. I am returning to Glom immediately - alone. The Third Planet is a dangerous place. Don't send any more spaceships here. See you in fifteen years.

Space Commander Zook

The outback

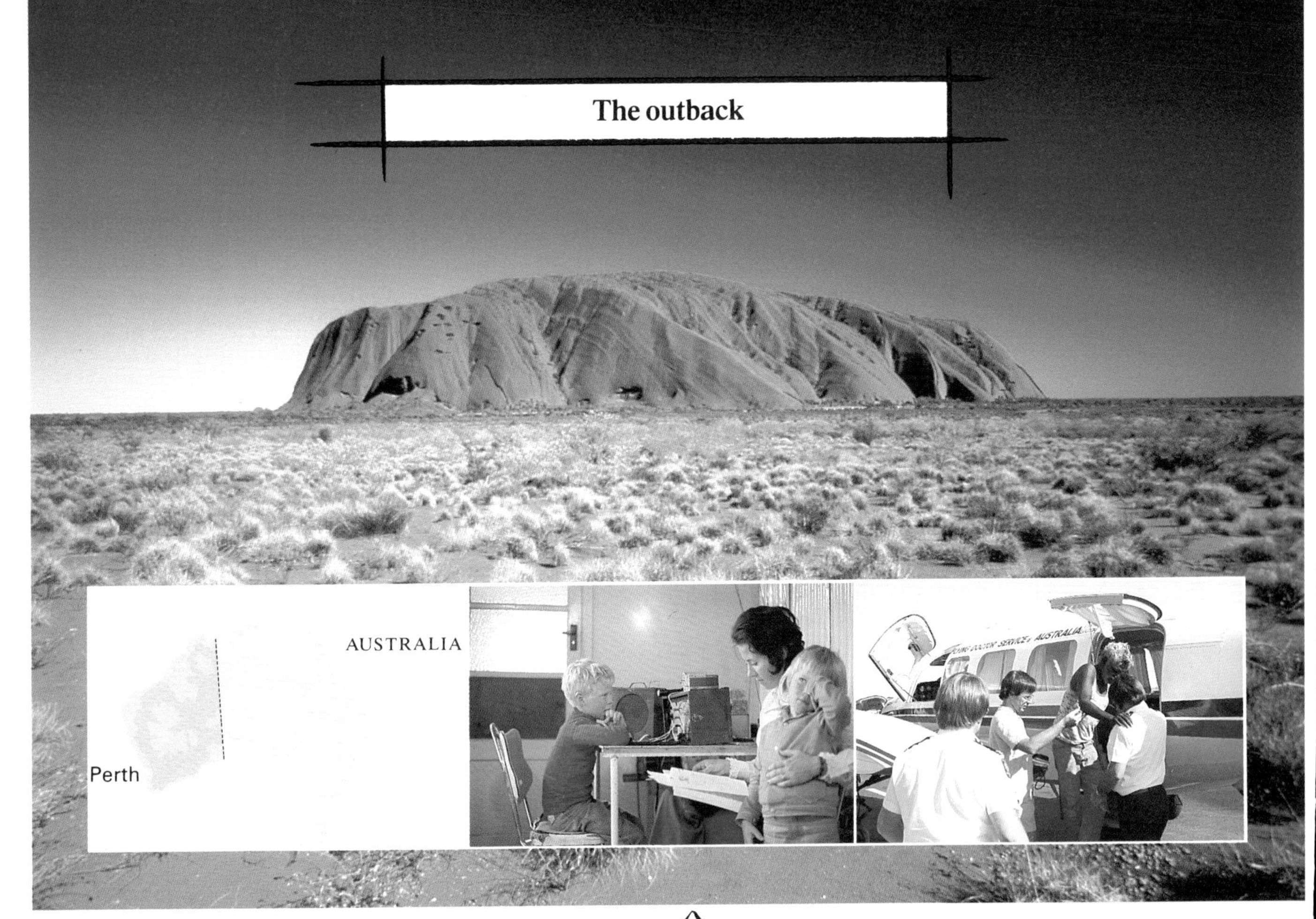

Western Australia is eight times the size of Britain, but it has only one million people. 900,000 of them live in and around the state capital, Perth. The other 100,000 people live in 'the outback', an area of 2,500,000 square kilometres. The area is hot and dry. Temperatures are usually over 30°C in summer, and sometimes over 40°C. It hardly ever rains. Sheep farming is the main occupation, and the farms are called 'sheep stations' in Australia.

Life on a sheep station is very different from life in a town. Houses are sometimes hundreds of kilometres from towns. Some people never go to towns, and never see shops. The sheep stations are very big, and children often ride motor bikes and drive cars.

The children can't go to school, and they hardly ever see a teacher. They have lessons from a two-way radio. It's called 'The School of the Air'. The students can speak to the teacher and other children in the class by radio. They get work by post. The post doesn't come very often, about once a week. Letter-boxes are on the roads, sometimes five or six kilometres from the houses.

There aren't any schools or shops in the outback, but what about doctors? People can talk to doctors by radio, and in an emergency a doctor comes to them by plane. They are called the 'Flying Doctors'.

a Facts about Western Australia

1 Complete this chart.

Area: ______

Summer temperature: ______

Population of state: ______

Capital: ______

Population of capital area: ______

Population of outback: ______

Main occupation: ______

2 Complete these sentences.
Put *usually, often, sometimes, hardly ever,* or *never* in the spaces.

1 Children in the outback ____ see a teacher.
2 They ____ talk to the teacher by radio.
3 The post ____ comes once a week.
4 The letter-boxes are ____ five or six kilometres from the houses.
5 Children ____ drive cars on the sheep stations.
6 Children ____ drive cars in the towns.
7 People ____ see a doctor.
8 Some people ____ go to towns.
9 The summer temperature is ____ over 30°C.
10 It ____ rains.

b What's it called?

Some words are different in Australia.
Answer these questions.

1 What is the 'country outside the towns' called?
2 What are large sheep farms called?
3 What is the radio school called?
4 What are the doctors called?

c Australian words

A *What's a mosquito called in Australia?*
B *It's called a 'mossie'.*

Ask and answer about the words in the lists.

Australian [Oz]	British English [Pom]
Aussie	Australian
brekky	breakfast
dingo	wild dog
fish 'n' greasies	fish 'n' chips
mossie	mosquito
Oz	Australia
Pom / Pommie	British person
postie	postman / postwoman

d What's this in English?

What's this (called) in English? / your language?
What are these (called) in English? / your language?

Ask and answer about the names of things in your classroom.

e The weather

It is usually hot and dry.
It hardly ever rains.

1 Describe the weather in Western Australia.
2 Talk about the weather in:
your country / North Africa / Northern Canada / Southern Europe / Eastern Europe / Britain.
Use these words: *always, usually, often, sometimes, hardly ever, never.*

always	
usually	
often	
sometimes	
hardly ever	
never	

f Questionnaire

1 Ask another student the questions.
Put a tick [✓] for his/her answers.

Questionnaire

1 Do you usually come to school
☐ by bus? ☐ by train? ☐ by car? ☐ by bike? ☐ on foot? ☐ other?

2 Do you see other students at weekends?
☐ always ☐ usually ☐ often ☐ sometimes ☐ hardly ever ☐ never

3 How often do you listen to records in English?
☐ often ☐ sometimes ☐ hardly ever ☐ never

4 How often do you listen to radio programmes?
☐ often ☐ sometimes ☐ hardly ever ☐ never

5 How often do you speak English outside school?
☐ often ☐ sometimes ☐ hardly ever ☐ never

6 Do you watch television in the evenings?
☐ always ☐ usually ☐ often ☐ sometimes ☐ hardly ever ☐ never

2 Talk to another student about your first partner's answers.

g Snacks survey

Julie is a market researcher. She does surveys by telephone. She's talking to a man.
This is the survey form. Tick [✓] his answers.

Snacks Survey
(for Chockie Bars)

Telephone Surveys plc
Market researcher : Julie Satchi
Call number : 15

Sex ☐ M ☐ F

1 How often do you eat between meals?
☐ often ☐ sometimes ☐ hardly ever ☐ never

2 Do you eat any of these things between meals?
☐ fruit ☐ nuts ☐ crisps ☐ biscuits ☐ chocolate

3 When do you usually have snacks?
☐ mornings ☐ afternoons ☐ evenings ☐ in the night

4 Where do you eat snacks?
☐ at home ☐ at school / the office ☐ in the street
☐ at the cinema

5 How often do you *buy* snacks?
☐ every day ☐ two or three times a week ☐ at weekends
☐ hardly ever

6 Do you know these makes of chocolate?
☐ Nestlé ☐ Suchard ☐ Hershey ☐ Cadbury ☐ Mars
☐ Chockie Bar

7 Would you like a free Chockie Bar? (We can send it by post.)
☐ Yes ☐ No

Tracey's first day

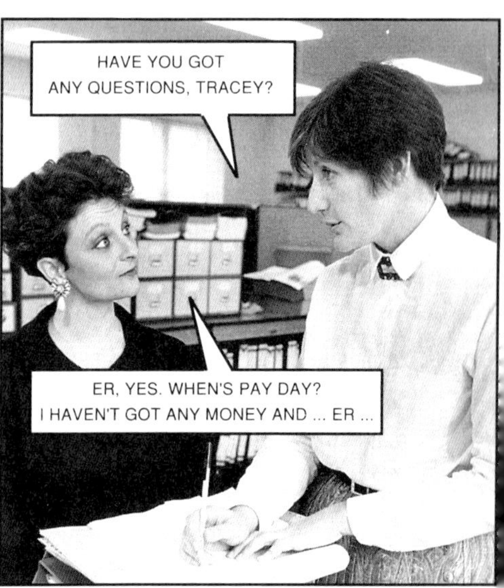

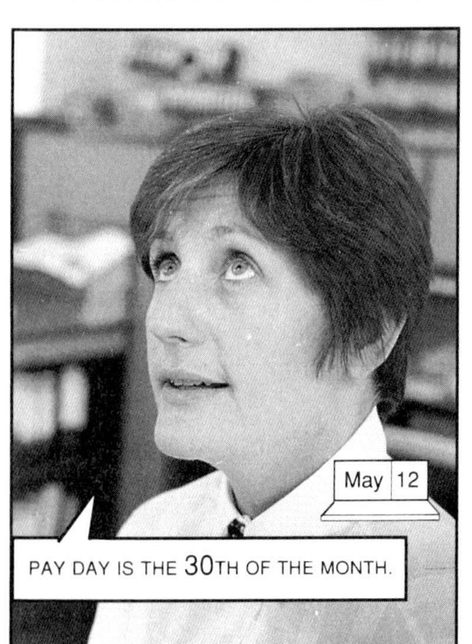

The past of *be*

was is the past of *is* and *am*.

Where was it? — *It wasn't here. / It was there.*

Was it in the bag? — *Yes, it was. / No, it wasn't.*

were is the past of *are*.

Where were they? — *They weren't in the office. They were at lunch.*

Were they in the restaurant? — *Yes, they were. No, they weren't.*

a Questions

Ask and answer.

1 Where was Mrs Steele / Mandy / Tracey / Mr Newbury at 9 o'clock?
2 Where were they at lunch-time?
3 Where were they at 2 o'clock?
4 Whose money was in Tracey's bag?
Where was Mr Newbury's money?

b Yesterday

1 Talk about yesterday.
Where were you yesterday?
Where were you in the morning / afternoon / evening?
Where were you at 8 o'clock / 11.30 / lunch-time / 3 o'clock / 6 o'clock / 10 o'clock / midnight?
Who was with you?

Ask another student.

2 Work with a different student.
Where was he/she yesterday?
Where was he/she in the morning / afternoon / evening?
Who was with him/her?

Ask about this student's first partner.

Beware of pickpockets!

Inspector Franklin works for the Metropolitan Police at London's Heathrow Airport. He's talking to his police officers now.

Inspector OK. This man's name is Brian Smith. This is an Identikit picture of him. Remember his face. He's a pickpocket. He always works at airports and seaports. He steals money, credit cards, and passports from travellers. People are usually careful at airports, but in the departure lounges they're sometimes careless. They think they're OK. Now, we've got some police reports about Mr Smith.

Listen. Yesterday morning he was in Aberdeen. There were six robberies at the airport. He was at Heathrow at nine o'clock. There were five robberies. At lunch-time he was in Paris ... five robberies again. Then at two o'clock he was at a railway station in Paris. There were seven robberies.

There were four robberies at the Hovercraft port in Boulogne just before five o'clock French time, one at Dover at five o'clock English time – and two robberies at Victoria Station in London at seven. Last night there were more robberies here at Heathrow. He was on the last flight to Manchester last night.

Policeman But sir, it's impossible! In one day he was in seven places!

Inspector It's *not* impossible. Look at the timetables!

Policeman What was he wearing yesterday?

Inspector He was wearing a long coat, and a hat. He was also wearing glasses yesterday. Last week he was in Amsterdam, and he wasn't wearing glasses then. His hair was short and blond yesterday. But last week it was brown, and last month it was long and black. Last year it was grey.

Policeman It's going to be impossible, sir.

Inspector Not impossible ... but it *is* going to be difficult!

a Timetables

Look at the timetables. Which flights was he on? Which trains? Which hovercraft?

From MANCHESTER
Depart Manchester Airport (see Minimum Check-in Times for UK)
Reservations tel 061 2286311

→ ABERDEEN

From	To	Days 1234567	Depart	Arrive	Flight No.	Air-craft	Class	Stops
		12345 --	0820	0920	BA5690	B11	M	0
		1 --- 5 --	1225	1350	BA5694	HPJ	M	0
		-234 ---	1455	1620	BA5696	HPJ	M	0
		1 --- 5 --	1615	1740	BA5698	HPJ	M	0
		12345 --	1835	2000	BA5688	HS7	M	0
		------ 7	1910	2130	BA867	HS7	M	1

Paris to London (rail/hovercraft)

PERIOD OF OPERATION		A	DAILY	DAILY
Paris Nord	d	0920	1125	1420
Boulogne Hoverport	d	1205	1405	1705
SEA CROSSING		⛴	⛴	⛴
Dover Hoverport	a	1145	1345	1645
London Victoria	a	1353	1553	1853

ALL TIMES SHOWN ARE LOCAL

⛴ Hoverspeed hovercraft with in-flight bar service.
Advance reservation essential. Trains for hovercraft services arrive at and depart from Dover Priory.
A free bus service connects Dover Priory with Dover Hoverport in both directions.

From ABERDEEN

→ PARIS (Via LONDON HEATHROW)

From	To	Days 1234567	Depart	Arrive	Flight No.	Air-craft	Class	Stops	Transfer Arr.	Airport	Dep.	Flight
		12345 --	1005	1400	BA992	811	CM	1				
		1 ------	1015	1430	BA5607	737	M	1	1140	LHR	1230	BA308
		Daily	1105	1630	BA5609	73S	M	1	1230	LHR	1430	BA312
		123456 -	1400	1830	BA5611	737	M	1	1525	LHR	1630	BA314
		12345 - 7	1535	2030	BA5613	73S	M	1	1700	LHR	1830	BA316
		12345 - 7	1730	2200	BA5615	757	M	1	1855	LHR	2000	BA318

From LONDON

→ MANCHESTER

From	To	Days 1234567	Depart	Arrive	Flight No.	Air-craft	Class	Stops
		12345 --	0730①	0820	BA4402	757	M	0
		Daily	0930①	1020	BA4422	757	M	0
		Daily	1130①	1220	BA4442	757	M	0
		Daily	1330①	1420	BA4462	757	M	0
		Daily	1630①	1720	BA4492	757	M	0
		Daily	1830①	1920	BA4512	757	M	0
		Daily	2030①	2120	BA4532	757	M	0

From LONDON

→ PARIS

From	To	Days 1234567	Depart	Arrive	Flight No.	Air-craft	Class	Stops
		123456 -	0640 ①	0840	BA302	757	CM	0
		123 - 56 -	0730 ②	0930	AF807	AB3	CY	0
		Daily	0830 ①	1030	BA304	L10	CM	0
	20 Dec	Daily	0930 ②	1130	AF809	AB3	CY	0
22 Dec		12345 - 7	0930 ②	1130	AF809	AB3	CY	0
		Daily	1030 ①	1230	BA306	757	CM	0

From ABERDEEN

→ LONDON

From	To	Days 1234567	Depart	Arrive	Flight No.	Air-craft	Class	Stops
		12345 --	0700	0825	BA5601	757	M	0
		-----67	0800	0925	BA5603	737	M	0
		12345 --	0940	1105	BA5605	737	M	0
		1 ------	1015	1140	BA5607	737	M	0
		Daily	1105	1230	BA5609	73S	M	0
		123456 -	1400	1525	BA5611	737	M	0
		12345 -7	1535	1700	BA5613	73S	M	0
		Daily	1730	1855	BA5615	757	M	0
		12345 --	1945	2110	BA5619	73S	M	0

b Identikit

Yesterday the name in his passport was Brian Smith. Last week it was Clive Jones. Look at these identikit pictures.

Last week.
Clive Jones.
Amsterdam.

Last month.
Clive Smith.
Rome.

Last year.
Brian Jones.
New York.

What was his name last week?
Where was he?
What was he like?
Ask and answer about the identikit pictures.

c What was he wearing?

1 Student A: What was he wearing last week? What do *you* think? Write a list.
Student B: Ask questions about last week.
2 Do the same for last month and last year.

d Two other pickpockets

Inspector Franklin is looking for two other pickpockets. They were in Manchester, Aberdeen, Paris, and London yesterday.
They were in Manchester at 7 o'clock.
There was one robbery. etc.
Use the timetables and make more sentences.

A good dinner

Man Hello, Mrs Cole?
Mrs Cole Yes?
Man I'm from the Public Health Department.
Mrs Cole Oh, yes?
Man Can I ask you a few questions?
Mrs Cole Well, yes ...
Man Did you go to the supermarket this morning?
Mrs Cole Yes. Yes, I did.
Man Which supermarket did you go to?
Mrs Cole I went to Safebury's. I always go to Safebury's.
Man Ah, Safebury's! Did you go to the branch in the High Street?
Mrs Cole Yes, I did.
Man Oh dear. When did you go there?
Mrs Cole I went at 9 o'clock this morning.

Man Did you buy any beef?
Mrs Cole No, I didn't buy any beef. I don't like beef.
Man Oh. Did you buy *any* meat?
Mrs Cole Meat? Yes, I did. I bought some chicken.
Man Chicken? Good. Have you got it now?
Mrs Cole Yes, it's in the fridge.
Man Can you get it, please?
Mrs Cole What? I don't understand. Why ...?
Man You can't eat it, Mrs Cole. Five people have got food poisoning. They all bought meat at Safebury's.

Mrs Cole Oh dear. It was very expensive. It was seven pounds fifty.
Man Don't worry, Mrs Cole. Safebury's are going to send you a cheque for fifteen pounds.
Mrs Cole Well, that's all right, then.
Man I'm going to take the chicken. It's going to our laboratory.
Mrs Cole Oh! Oh, yes ... well, thank you.
Man Thank *you*, Mrs Cole.

Woman Did you get any beef?
Man No, I didn't. But I got some chicken.
Woman Great!
Man What did you get?
Woman I got some fish at number 23, and some chocolate cake from Mrs Roberts at number 14.
Man Right, we've got dinner. Let's go home!
Policeman Excuse me ...
Woman Oh no! The police ...

a Mrs Cole's shopping list

This is Mrs Cole's shopping list for this morning. She didn't get everything. A tick [✓] means she got it. A cross [✗] means she didn't get it.

Safebury's	Chemist	Baker
Chicken ✓	Toothpaste ✓	Bread ✓
Potatoes ✓	Toothbrush ✗	Cakes ✗
Washing-up liquid ✓	Aspirins ✓	Rolls ✓
Tuna fish ✗		
Apple Juice ✗		

Look at the list.
Did she go to . . .?
Did she buy . . .? / Did she get . . .?
Ask and answer about Mrs Cole's list.

b Your shopping list

1 Write a shopping list.
Say *This is my shopping list for yesterday*.
Put a tick [*I bought it*] or a cross [*I didn't buy it*] next to the things on the list.
2 Work with another student.
Ask questions, and find out what's on his/her list.
Which shops did he/she go to? What did he/she buy?

c Questions

Ask and answer.
1 Where did you go last weekend?
2 Did you go to the shops?
3 Did you buy anything?
4 What did you buy?
5 Did you get any letters yesterday?
6 How many did you get?

d Questionnaire

A *Did you have a bath yesterday?*
B *No, I didn't have a bath. I had a shower.*

Ask another student about yesterday.
Underline the answers.
Sometimes the true answer isn't on the chart.
Ask questions with: *Where? When? What time? What?*

Breakfast	before 8.00? tea?	at 8.00? coffee?	after 8.00? fruit juice?
Lunch	at home? at 12.00?	in a restaurant? at 1.00?	at school / work? at 2.00?
Dinner	at home? beef?	in a restaurant? chicken?	at a friend's house? fish?
Bath / shower	bath? in the morning?	shower? in the afternoon?	wash? in the evening?

e Jigsaw

There are five paragraphs in this story. They are in the wrong order.
Number them in the correct order, from 1 to 5.

The next morning there was a knock on the door. Sid went to the door. A policewoman was outside.
'Mr Cole?' she said.
'Mr Sidney Cole?'
'Er...yes, that's me,' said Sid.
'Were you on the M40 last night at about eleven o'clock?'
'No,' said Sid. 'No, I wasn't. Not me.'
'Could I see your car please?' said the policewoman.

Just then there was a terrible noise behind them. Two cars crashed, then a third car, then a fourth. The policemen ran to the accident. Sid was alone beside the motorway. He waited for a moment, then he got into the Jaguar and went home...very fast. He put the car into his garage, closed the door, went into his house, and went to bed.

Sid Cole bought a new white Jaguar last week. He got the car last Friday, and that evening he went out for a drive. The Jaguar was very fast, and Sid was going along the M40 motorway at 100mph. Suddenly, there was a blue light behind him, a blue flashing light. It was a police car.

They went to the garage. Sid opened the door. There was a white Jaguar in the garage, but it wasn't his Jaguar. There were red and yellow stripes on the side, and a blue light on the roof. And it had the word **POLICE** on the door.

Sid stopped, and the police car stopped next to him. It was a Jaguar too.
'Get out of your car,' said a policeman. Sid did. He was cold. It was a cold, dark December night. There were two policemen. They were very angry.
'Do you know the speed limit?' said one.
'Yes,' said Sid. '70mph. I'm sorry. It's a new car and...'

One dark night

1

Barry and Jenny are on holiday. It's ten o'clock in the evening. They're on a dark and lonely country road. Their car stops . . .

Jenny What's wrong with it?
Barry I don't know.
Jenny Is there any petrol?
Barry Yes. I put some in this afternoon. I got thirty litres.
Jenny What are we going to do?
Barry I'm going to find a telephone.
Jenny I'm coming with you.
Barry No, it's freezing! You wait here.
Jenny Barry, I'm frightened . . .

2

Later.

Barry Jenny . . . it's me. Open the door! Sorry. Did I frighten you?
Jenny No. Did you find a telephone?
Barry No, I didn't find a telephone . . . But I found a hotel. I went round that corner and I saw it. They've got a room for tonight. We can phone a garage tomorrow. Come on . . .

3

They're in the hotel room.

Barry Well, what do you think?
Jenny I don't like it.

He goes into the bathroom. There's a noise outside.

Jenny Barry! Did you hear that?
Barry What?
Jenny I heard something. It was a laugh. It was horrible.
Barry I didn't hear anything.
Jenny You were in the bathroom.
Barry Yes, and there aren't any towels. I'm going down to reception.
Jenny OK.
Barry Don't worry, Jenny. I'm not frightened.

4

Barry Jenny!
Jenny What's the matter?
Barry I went outside . . . and I saw someone in the corridor. He was wearing a long black cloak . . . like Count Dracula.
Jenny Don't be silly, Barry. I *was* frightened, but I'm not stupid.
Barry He was there! I saw him. He had big teeth, and . . .
Jenny This isn't funny, Barry.
Barry Look . . . he went round the corner. And I went after him . . . and there wasn't anyone there.
Jenny What?
Barry I didn't see anyone.

5

Jenny What did you say?
Barry I didn't say anything, there was a noise. Be quiet!
Jenny Barry! That was you!
Barry I said 'Be quiet'! Did you hear that? Come on! I'm not staying here . . . Let's go. .

Irregular verbs

PRESENT	PAST
find	found
see	saw
hear	heard
put	put
say	said

a On the way here

On the way to this lesson:

Did you see ☐ a police car ☐ a dog ☐ any trees ☐ the teacher ☐ a boat?
What did you see?

Did you hear ☐ an ambulance ☐ a plane ☐ a radio ☐ someone singing?
What did you hear?

Did you find ☐ any money on the street ☐ anything?

Did you put any of these things in your bag / briefcase this morning?
☐ money ☐ food ☐ chewing-gum ☐ make-up ☐ a toothbrush
What did you put in your bag this morning?

Ask and answer with another student.

b A noise in the night

Complete the spaces with *something*, *someone*, *anything*, or *anyone*.

It was very dark. I found my watch on the table next to my bed. Three o'clock! Then I heard ______ downstairs. What was it? I got out of bed, and went out of the room. I went to the stairs. Then I saw ______ . Was it a light? Carefully, I went downstairs. I didn't say ______ . I was very quiet. Then I heard ______ . It was a woman. 'I'm going to kill him, give me the gun!' she said. I didn't move. Then I heard music.
'Is ______ there?' I said. I heard music again.
I went into the living room. There wasn't ______ there, but the television was on! The video recorder has got an automatic timer. Before I went to bed I put the timer on for three o'clock the next afternoon. I went to the video. The timer was on for three o'clock in the morning.

One of them was wearing high-heeled shoes. She was an old American lady with white hair. I didn't say anything. Her husband had four or five cameras and a big hat. There were two English ladies in their seventies, three boys from New Zealand and a young Canadian couple. They got into the boat.
Ray wasn't there. He was late again. It was hot, very hot - about 32 °C - and it was only ten o'clock.
'When are we leaving?' said the American lady.
'I don't know,' I said. 'We're waiting for the captain.'

They found seats and waited in the sun. The Canadians didn't have any hats. I got two old hats from the back of the boat.
'Here,' I said; 'you're going to need these. It's going to be hot out there.'
They put them on.
'The advertisement said ten o'clock,' said the American man.
'Yes?' I said. 'Well, we usually leave at ten. Today we're late. Sorry.'

Then I saw Ray. He was running towards the boat. He was wearing his white suit, and his face was red. He got onto the boat, and it went down a long way into the water. Ray's a very fat man.
'G'day,' he said. 'It's a nice morning.'
'Good day,' said the tourists. I smiled. In Australian films people always say 'G'day', but the tourists didn't have the right accent.
'G'day Ray,' I said. I was doing my job. Tourists want to see Australia, and hear Australians. That's my job. I'm a professional Australian. What next? Yeah, a joke. Australians always make jokes.
'Did you have a good breakfast, Ray?' I said.
'Yeah,' said Ray. 'Why?'
'I can see it on your jacket. You had eggs, tomatoes, and coffee, right?'

Ray was angry about that one. His jacket *was* dirty. His clothes are always dirty. His boat's dirty, too. Last month I said,
'Ray, why don't you clean the boat?'
'Look,' he said; 'tourists want a journey through the jungle. A dirty boat has got the

right . . . the right . . . ambience.
'What's ambience?' I said. 'You know me, Ray. I'm just a crocodile hunter. I don't understand difficult words.'
Ray doesn't like me, but then I don't like him. But it's a job. I started the old engine and we went up the river.

It's a two-hour journey into the jungle. The tourists bought drinks from Ray. He always sells them warm Pepsi-Cola, at a very high price. Ray talks about the jungle on the journey. And me? I sit at the back of the boat and sleep.
'There they are!' shouted the American woman. I opened one eye. There were some big crocs at the side of the river. They were asleep. They always wake up when the boat goes past. One big old croc came into the river. All the tourists had their cameras. The American man was taking photographs. Ray was in the middle of the talk.
'Yes, crocodiles sometimes eat people,' he said. 'In this part of Australia they eat three or four people every year.'
I smiled. Was it true? I don't know. But the tourists love the stories.
We got to the Tickabaree River, and Ray turned the boat into it.
'But don't worry,' he said. 'Mr Preston is a professional crocodile hunter. He's got his gun.' Ray was looking at me.
'He's got his *gun*,' he said again.
I found the gun at the bottom of the boat. The tourists looked at me.
'Do you need that gun?' said one of the Canadians.
'Oh, yes,' said Ray. 'Sometimes the crocodiles attack small boats.'
The tourists went quiet, very quiet.

I saw the big tree. We were at the right place. I put my hand on a small electric control next to the engine.
The crocodile came out of the water right in front of the boat. Water came into the boat.
'Aargh!' It was the American woman.
'The gun!' said Ray. 'Quick!'
I pulled the trigger. 'Oh no!' I shouted. 'The gun! There's something wrong with the gun!'
Then I was in the water. I had my knife in my hand. I put my arm round the crocodile. We went under the water. Then I came out of the water with the crocodile and then went under again. The tourists were screaming and shouting.
I came out of the water again, and smiled. I had the crocodile's foot in my hand. It was the end of the show.

Tourists always love it. The electric control operates the plastic crocodile. They're afraid, but then they see it's a joke.
But Ray was shouting. 'Get her! Get her!'
'I've got her!' I said.
'Not the crocodile,' he said; 'the American woman! Look!'

The old American woman was in the river. The high-heeled shoes! You never wear high-heeled shoes on a small boat. I went towards her.

'She can't swim!' shouted her husband.
The water in the Tickabaree River is only about one metre deep, but she was afraid. I got her arms, then I heard Ray again.
'Preston! Be careful! There's a crocodile!'
'Very funny,' I shouted.
'No, behind you! There's a crocodile!'
It wasn't a joke. There it was, a big old croc about two metres away, and it wasn't a plastic one this time. The American woman was in my arms. Then the crocodile was next to us. I didn't have my knife now. I saw its cold eyes and its big teeth. It had a lot of teeth. Then I hit the crocodile. I hit it once on the nose. Was Ray's story true? Do they eat three or four people a year? Was I on the menu for today?

Then the crocodile went. It turned and went away. I was at the boat. They helped us into the boat. Perhaps that old croc just wasn't hungry, or maybe it didn't like me. I don't know, but I was a hero. Me, a hero!

The plastic crocodile isn't in the Tickabaree River any more. The next day Ray put it outside his office. It's an advert for the boat journeys. I don't go in the river now. I was lucky that time, but maybe next time . . . who knows?

The Morgans

Wally Morgan wanted to know about his ancestors. He looked in old books, and visited churches. He discovered a lot of things about his family.

Wallace Morgan was a pirate. He lived from 1624 to 1657. He worked as a navigator for Captain Elijah Blood. They sailed round the world three times between 1646 and 1657. This was by mistake: Wallace didn't have a map. Finally, in 1657 they arrived in England. Wallace died in his bath. He slipped on the soap and drowned.

His grandfather, Willy Morgan, played football for England. He was a defender. He played against Scotland in 1923. The game started at 3 o'clock on a Saturday afternoon in May. England scored the first goal at 4.15. Then Willy scored two goals . . . both of them for Scotland. He didn't play for England again.

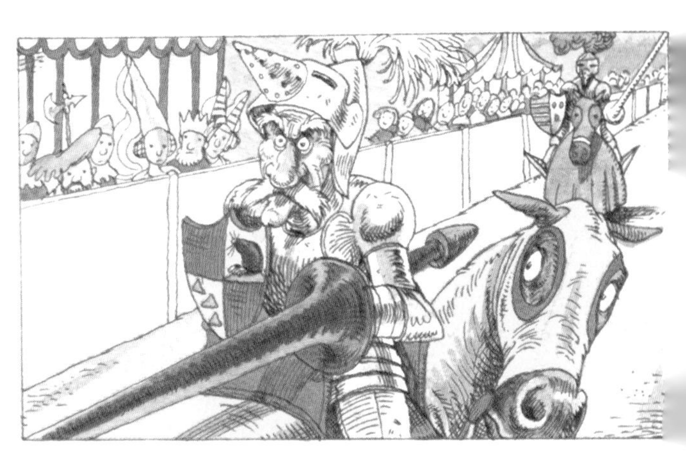

Sir William Morgan lived from 1413 to 1452. He was very romantic. He loved Lady Matilda Potter, the niece of the King. He wanted to marry her. He asked her to marry him in 1432. She said 'No'. He asked her again in 1437, 1441, 1443, and 1450. Finally, she married him in 1452. He died ten minutes after the wedding. His horse stopped on a bridge. He fell off and landed in the river. He was wearing his armour. It weighed 400 kilograms.

Billy 'Four Eyes' Morgan lived from 1857 to 1886. He moved to the United States in 1879, and in 1886 he was the Sheriff of Rattlesnake County. He died in a gunfight with Jesse James. Billy fired his gun six times, but he didn't kill Jesse. He killed three horses, a dog, the State Governor, and a Deputy Sheriff. Then Jesse killed him. Billy wasn't wearing his glasses.

a What happened?

Work with another student.
Make questions and answers about the stories.

Regular verbs: spellings

In English, some verbs are **irregular** in the past:
went, saw, got, bought, fell, etc.

Some verbs are **regular**:
add *-ed*, or *-d* to the present.

Remember these spelling rules:

add *-d*:
move, fire, live, die – moved etc.

add *-ed*:
want, visit, kill, sail – wanted etc.

change *y* to *ied*:
marry – married, hurry – hurried etc.

double the consonant:
slip – slipped, stop – stopped etc.

b Regular verbs: sounds

-d and *-ed* have three different sounds. Sometimes they sound like [t], sometimes they sound like [d], sometimes they sound like [ɪd]. Listen to the cassette. Look at the verbs below, and put a tick [✓] in the correct place.

verb	[t]	[d]	[ɪd]
wanted			
looked			
visited			
discovered			
played			
started			
scored			
lived			
moved			
died			
fired			
killed			
worked			
sailed			
arrived			
slipped			
drowned			
loved			
asked			
married			
stopped			
landed			
weighed			

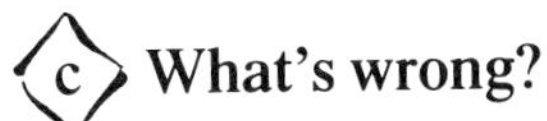

c What's wrong?

Picture **1** *They didn't have knives and forks in 100,000 BC.*
or *They didn't eat with knives and forks in 100,000 BC.*

Having a conversation

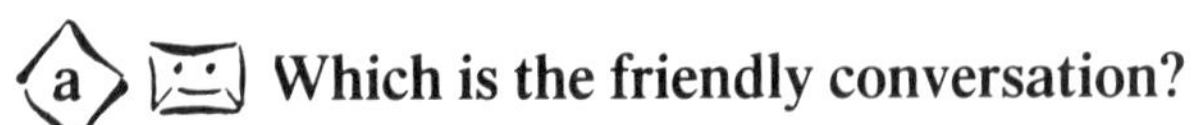

(a) Which is the friendly conversation?

In English, the **sound** is very important. You can sound friendly, you can sound interested, you can sound happy, you can sound angry, or you can sound afraid.

1 Look at these sentences. Which is the friendly one?
- *Yes, thanks.*
- *Yes, thank you very much. You're very kind.*

Answer:

You don't know. You can't hear the sound.

2 You're going to hear some pairs of conversations. Which is the friendly conversation – conversation A, or conversation B? Put a tick [✓] in the boxes below.

Conversation

1	A ☐	B ☐	**4**	A ☐	B ☐
2	A ☐	B ☐	**5**	A ☐	B ☐
3	A ☐	B ☐	**6**	A ☐	B ☐

(b) Starting a conversation

How do you start and continue a conversation? There's a right way, and a wrong way! Listen to these two conversations. Which is the right way? Why?

☐ Er . . . It's not very nice today, is it?
☐ No, it isn't. Not very nice at all.
☐ It's very cold . . . for Spring.
☐ Mmm. The weather forecast was rain for tonight.
☐ Was it? Well, it's usually wrong!
☐ Yes, but not always. The forecast on Saturday was fog, and it was foggy all day.

☐ 'Morning. It's a nice day, isn't it?
☐ Yes.
☐ Is it going to rain later?
☐ I don't know.
☐ Oh.

Some ways to start and continue a conversation:

1 In England, talk about the weather.
2 Smile.
3 Sound friendly. Sound interested.
4 Look at the other person. Listen to them.
5 Don't stop the conversation. Answer. Then ask questions.
6 Give more information.

(c) Conversations about the weather

Make conversations about the weather. Use some of these words:

wonderful lovely nice
not very nice awful terrible

hot warm cool cold
wet dry foggy cloudy sunny

snow rain fog sunshine

to rain to snow to thunder
to be hot / warm / cool / etc

spring summer autumn winter
January / July / etc

d Talking about interests and hobbies

1 What do you like doing? Ask another student.

Do you like:

_____ reading?	_____ swimming?
_____ playing sports?	_____ travelling?
_____ listening to music?	_____ going to the cinema?
_____ dancing?	_____ watching videos?
_____ collecting things?	

Ask more questions like these.

2 What kind? Look at the pictures.

A *Do you like reading?*
B *Yes, I do. Very much.*

A *What kind of books do you like?*
B *I like books about animals, and I enjoy science fiction, too.*
A *What's your favourite book?*
B *I don't know . . .* Lord of the Rings, *I think.*

Make more conversations.

e Telling stories

In long conversations we often tell stories or jokes. Here are some examples.

A true story

I heard a story about a woman in England. One day she saw a large truck outside her neighbours' house. Anyway, she was surprised because her neighbours were on holiday. Then some men came out of her neighbours' door. They had her neighbours' valuable Persian carpets. They put them into the truck. The woman went over to the men and said, 'What are you doing with those carpets?'
'We're taking them to the cleaner's,' said one of the men.
'That's wonderful,' she said. 'Can you take my carpets too?'
'All right,' said the man, and they took her carpets to the truck.
Anyway, she never saw them again. The men were burglars.

A joke

A little boy came home after his first day at school. 'What did you do today?' said his mother.
'We did some writing,' said the little boy.
'That's nice. What did you write?' said his mother.
'I don't know,' said the little boy, 'We didn't do reading.'

Tell another student a story or a joke.

OOKS

animals

travel

science fiction

novels

romantic novels

detective stories

LMS / DEOS

science fiction

war / adventure

comedy

horror

westerns

musicals

drama

USIC

pop

rock

soul / disco

classical

jazz

folk

PORT

ming

walking

riding

play

football

volleyball

tennis

do

athletics

judo

aerobics

yoga

Going home

Doris and Harry Flint are English. They're on holiday in San Miguel. It's the last day of their holiday, and they're waiting for their bus to the airport.

Harry Oh dear. When will that bus be here? Look at the time!
Doris Don't worry, love. It'll be here soon.
Harry We'll be late.
Doris No, we won't.
Harry Yes, we will. We'll miss the plane.
Doris No, dear. We won't miss the plane.
Harry Are you sure, Doris?
Doris Yes, I'm sure, Harry. We'll be there on time.
Harry Will we?
Doris Yes. They won't leave without us.
Harry Well, they did last year. We were only ten minutes late. They left without us then.
Doris Well, we won't miss it this year. Here it comes now . . .
Harry Thank goodness for that!

(a) Questions

Ask and answer.
1 Will you be at school tomorrow?
2 Will you be at school on Saturday?
3 Will you be at school on Sunday?
4 Will you do any homework tonight?
5 What time will you go home tomorrow?
6 What time will you eat this evening?
7 What time will you go to bed?
8 What time will you get up tomorrow?
9 What time will you leave home tomorrow morning?

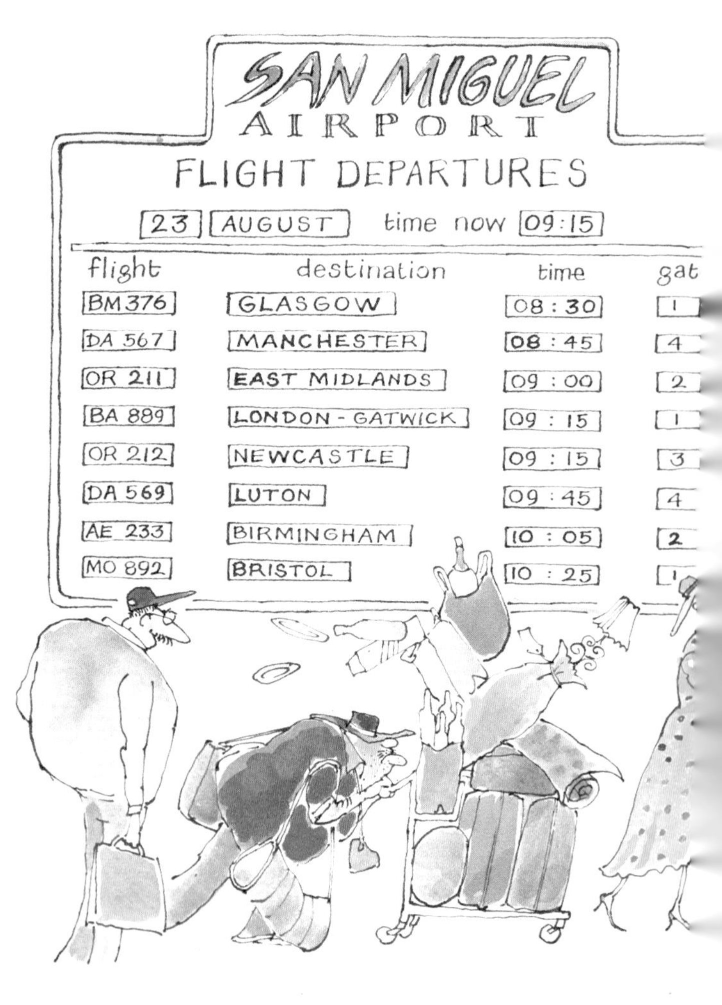

Present: It's 9.15. The flight to London-Gatwick is leaving now.
Past: The flight to East Midlands left at 9 o'clock.
Future: The flight to Luton will leave at 9.45.

(b) Flight departures

Make sentences about the flights to Glasgow, Manchester, Newcastle, Birmingham, and Bristol.

c You'll finish soon?

'll is sometimes difficult to hear.
Listen to the cassette. Which sentence can you hear?
Put a tick [✓] by the correct one.

1 ☐ I'll leave at 6 o'clock.
☐ I leave at 6 o'clock.
2 ☐ We'll arrive at 7.
☐ We arrive at 7.
3 ☐ They'll play football.
☐ They play football.
4 ☐ I'll have a bath at 8 o'clock.
☐ I have a bath at 8 o'clock.
5 ☐ You'll finish soon.
☐ You finish soon.
6 ☐ He'll put it there.
☐ He put it there.

Dates

1 / 12 Say *the first of December.*

Say these dates:

2 / 11	6 / 7	10 / 3
3 / 10	7 / 6	11 / 2
4 / 9	8 / 5	12 / 1
5 / 8	9 / 4	13 / 12

Frank and Betty

'rank and Betty are flight attendants. They got married ast year. Their jobs are a problem. He hardly ever sees ier, and she hardly ever sees him.
.ook at their timetables for next week.

ay	Frank	Betty
Ionday 11th	London – Paris	New York – London
uesday 12th	Paris – Rome	FREE (London)
'ednesday 13th	Rome – Dublin	FREE (London)
hursday 14th	Dublin – London	London – Miami
riday 15th	FREE (London)	Miami – New York
aturday 16th	FREE (London)	New York – London

A *Where will he be on Monday evening?*
B *He'll be in Paris.*
A *Where will she be?*
B *She'll be in London.*
A *Where will he go on Tuesday 12th?*
B *He'll go to Rome.*

Ask and answer about their week.

f The calendar

1 Look at the calendar. Put a ring around birthdays that are important for you.
(Your birthday, birthdays of family and friends.)

JANUARY ▸
1 2 3 4 5 6
7 8 9 10 11 12 13
14 15 16 17 18 19 20
21 22 23 24 25 26 27
28 29 30 31

FEBRUARY ▸
1 2 3
4 5 6 7 8 9 10
11 12 13 14 15 16 17
18 19 20 21 22 23 24
25 26 27 28 (29)

MARCH ▸
1 2 3
4 5 6 7 8 9 10
11 12 13 14 15 16 17
18 19 20 21 22 23 24
25 26 27 28 29 30 31

APRIL ▸
1 2 3 4 5 6 7
8 9 10 11 12 13 14
15 16 17 18 19 20 21
22 23 24 25 26 27 28
29 30

MAY ▸
1 2 3 4 5
6 7 8 9 10 11 12
13 14 15 16 17 18 19
20 21 22 23 24 25 26
27 28 29 30 31

JUNE ▸
1 2
3 4 5 6 7 8 9
10 11 12 13 14 15 16
17 18 19 20 21 22 23
24 25 26 27 28 29 30

JULY ▸
1 2 3 4 5 6 7
8 9 10 11 12 13 14
15 16 17 18 19 20 21
22 23 24 25 26 27 28
29 30 31

AUGUST ▸
1 2 3 4
5 6 7 8 9 10 11
12 13 14 15 16 17 18
19 20 21 22 23 24 25
26 27 28 29 30 31

SEPTEMBER ▸
1
2 3 4 5 6 7 8
9 10 11 12 13 14 15
16 17 18 19 20 21 22
23 24 25 26 27 28 29
30

OCTOBER ▸
1 2 3 4 5 6
7 8 9 10 11 12 13
14 15 16 17 18 19 20
21 22 23 24 25 26 27
28 29 30 31

NOVEMBER ▸
1 2 3
4 5 6 7 8 9 10
11 12 13 14 15 16 17
18 19 20 21 22 23 24
25 26 27 28 29 30

DECEMBER ▸
1
2 3 4 5 6 7 8
9 10 11 12 13 14 15
16 17 18 19 20 21 22
23 24 25 26 27 28 29
30 31

2 Work with another student. If today is June 9th, and there is a ring around March 3rd and November 22nd, you can make conversations like these:

March 3rd (PAST)

A *Whose birthday is March 3rd?*
B *It's my sister's birthday.*
A *How old was she?*
B *She was fourteen.*

November 22nd (FUTURE)

A *Whose birthday is November 22nd?*
B *It's my mother's birthday.*
A *How old will she be?*
B *She'll be thirty-nine.*

Ask and answer about important dates for you and your partner.

3 Now put a ring around national holidays, religious days, and saints' days, etc.

4 Work with another student.

A *What's important about April 23rd?*
B *It's St. George's Day.*
A *Why is there a ring around July 4th?*
B *It's American Independence Day.*

Ask and answer about the important dates.

Offers and suggestions

Offers of help

Man Don't worry, dear. I'll help you.
Lady Pardon?
Man It's a busy road, isn't it? Come on, I'll take you across.
Lady That's very kind of you, but . . .
Man Ah! Here's a space in the traffic. Let's go.
Lady Thank you, but . . .
Man Shall I carry your shopping bag? It's heavy, isn't it?
Lady Well, yes, but . . .
Man There you are!
Lady But I didn't want to cross the road!
Man What? Why didn't you tell me?
Lady You didn't listen!
Man Oh! Er . . . Shall I take you back?
Lady No, thank you!

Suggestions

Carol It's no good. It's broken.
Morris But it's Friday night! My favourite programmes are on Friday night.
Carol I know! Shall we go out?
Morris All right, then. Where shall we go?
Carol Shall we go to the cinema?
Morris Oh, no! I don't like the cinema.
Carol Why don't we go to a restaurant?
Morris No. That's too expensive.
Carol All right. Let's go and see some friends.
Morris We haven't got any friends.
Carol I know! The shops are open late on Fridays.
Morris I don't want to go shopping.
Carol Yes, you do. Shall we go and buy a new television?

Offers	Accepting	Refusing
I'll do it.	Yes, please.	No, thank you.
Shall I do it?	Thank you very much.	No, it's all right. I'll do it.
	That's very kind of you.	Thank you, but I can do it.
	That's very nice of you.	That's very kind, but no thanks.

Suggestions	Agreeing	Disagreeing
Shall we do it?	Yes, let's do it.	I don't like (that).
Let's do it.	That's a good idea.	No, I don't want to.
Why don't we do it?	Yes, OK.	No, thanks.
	Yes, all right.	

a Offer to help

A *I've got a headache.*
B *I'll get you an aspirin. / Shall I get you an aspirin?*
A *Yes. Thank you very much.*
No, thanks. I'll be all right soon.

Look at the pictures and continue.

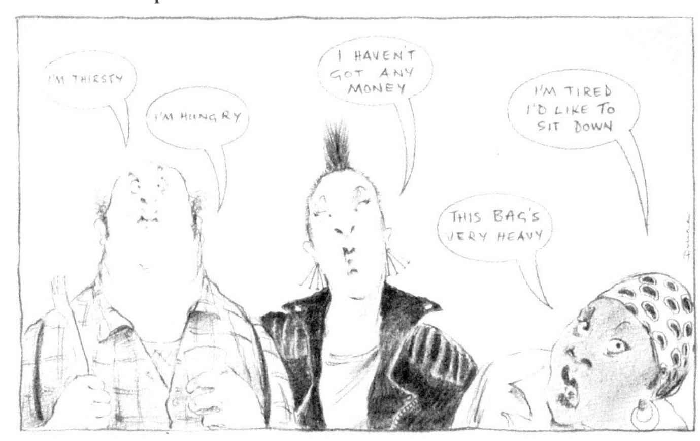

b Make suggestions

A *Shall we go to the cinema?*
B *Yes, that's a good idea. / No, I don't want to.*

Continue with these words: television / party / dancing / restaurant / disco / theatre / concert.

c Which film?

Look at these four conversations. They are all from films.
One conversation is from *True Hearts in Love*, one is from *Mrs Frankenstein*, one is from *Safari Hospital*, and one is from *Police School 6*.
Which conversation is from which film?

1 □ I'll help you, doctor. I'll help you ...
■ Hurry, she can't move her arm.
□ Shall I turn on the electricity?
■ Yes, we'll give her 50,000 volts.
□ She's moving, doctor. She's alive!

2 ■ But Antonia, I love you. I'll always love you!
■ It's no good, Cecil. Let's forget about it.
■ I'll do anything for you, Antonia.
■ Anything?
■ Anything.
■ Then go away from here. Go far away!

3 ■ Doctor! Hurry ... or we'll be too late.
Is that you, Adam? What's wrong?
■ It was an elephant, doctor. A mad elephant.
But I can't drive ... the fever ... I can't see ...
■ I'll drive you there, doctor. Shall we take the Land Rover?
The Land Rover? But Adam ... the brakes ... they don't ...

4 ■ There's someone in there. Let's phone for help.
■ There's no time. I'll go in.
■ Rod, you can't! You haven't got a gun.
■ I'll be all right. Why don't you phone for help?
■ No ... no, I'll come with you.
■ Thanks, Steve.

d Be a film star!

1 Act out the conversations from the films.
2 What happens next? Can you continue the conversation. Can you tell the story?

e Let's go to a movie

Shall we go to a movie?
Shall we go to a show?
Why don't we go somewhere quiet,
where the lights are soft and low?

I won't go to a movie,
I won't go to a show,
I won't go anywhere with you.
My answer will be 'No'.

Let's go to a party,
Let's go with the crowd.
Why don't we go to a disco,
where the music's playing loud?

I won't go to a disco,
I won't go to a show,
I won't go anywhere with you.
My answer will be 'No'.

I'll take you to the seaside.
Why don't we drive to the sea?
I'll take you to a lovely beach,
where there's only you and me.

I won't go to the seaside,
I won't go to a show,
I won't go anywhere with you.
My answer will be 'No'.

Treasure Island

Game

You will need something to score with:

You can use a dice. 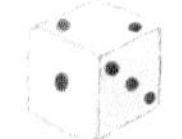

You can make a spinner.
You will need a piece of card and a pencil.

You can write the numbers on the six sides of a pencil. 

You can write the numbers on six pieces of paper.
Then fold the pieces, and mix them up.

You will need a counter:

You can use a coin, or any small object.

Rules

- Any number of players from 2 to 6 can play.
- You are on a desert island. The first person to get to the treasure is the winner.
  You need the *exact* number to get to the end.
  Each player throws the dice, and moves the correct number of spaces.
  Two or more players can be on the same space.
- Follow the arrows (➤ ➤ ➤). Each space has a number. Sometimes there will be an instruction.
  If you land on a red or yellow space, find the instruction in the list, and obey it.
- Red spaces. On the red spaces there are two paths, one to the left and one to the right. When you pass over a red space, read the instruction and continue in the direction it tells you. If you finish on a red space, read the instruction and go in that direction on your next throw.

You can take two things with you:

Choose two things from this list:
a map, a compass, a rope, an axe.
Write them down on a piece of paper.
On some spaces you get more things. You can have two of the same thing. Add a second one to your list.

Instructions

2 You find an axe on the beach. Add it to your list.
3 Have you got a map? YES – Go right; NO – Go left.
4 You remember there's a map on your boat.
Go back to 1, and add a map to your list.
6 You find a gold coin. Go forward to 14.
8 Did you walk here for this lesson?
YES – Go to 14; NO – Go to 7.
10 A crocodile attacks you. Go back to 5.
13 Is your birthday between the 1st and 15th of the month?
YES – Go forward one; NO – Go back to 2.
15 Is the first letter of your surname between A and M?
YES – Go back to 14; NO – Go on to 16.
17 Have you got an axe?
YES – Turn right, through the jungle; NO – Go left.
18 You kill a snake. Go forward to 21.
20 Have you got a compass or a rope?
You lose them in the jungle. Cross them off your list.
22 You find a rope. Add it to your list.
25 A snake bites you. Miss a turn.
27 Have you got a rope?
YES – Go left across the river; NO – Go right.
28 There is lava from the volcano on the path.
Wait until it's cold. Miss a turn.
30 You find a compass. Add it to your list.
32 You slip on the path and break your arm. Go back to 26.
34 You sit on your compass. It breaks. Cross it off your list.
36 You're frightened of the volcano. Go back to 26.
Your rope falls in the river. Cross it from your list.
38 You haven't got any food.
Go back to 21, and get some coconuts.
40 Did you have a hot drink with your breakfast?
YES – Go to 41; NO – Go to 39.
42 You are lost. Turn round and go to 33.
You find a compass on 33. Add it to your list.
43 Have you got a compass?
YES – Go west (to 48); NO – Go south (to 44).
44 You fall into the lake. The piranhas don't eat you, but go back to 41.
46 Can you swim 400 metres?
YES – Swim across to 56; NO – Stay on 46.
49 Will you stop studying English when you finish this book?
NO – Go forward to 53; YES – Go back to 41.
51 What are the past tenses of *go, buy, get*?
Three correct? – Go left (to 53);
Any wrong? Go right (fall down the cliff to 52).
54 Is your birthday between January 1st and June 30th?
YES – Go left (to 56); NO – Go right (to 55).
57 You're thirsty. Go back to 53 for water.
59 You think this is the wrong way. Go back to 50.

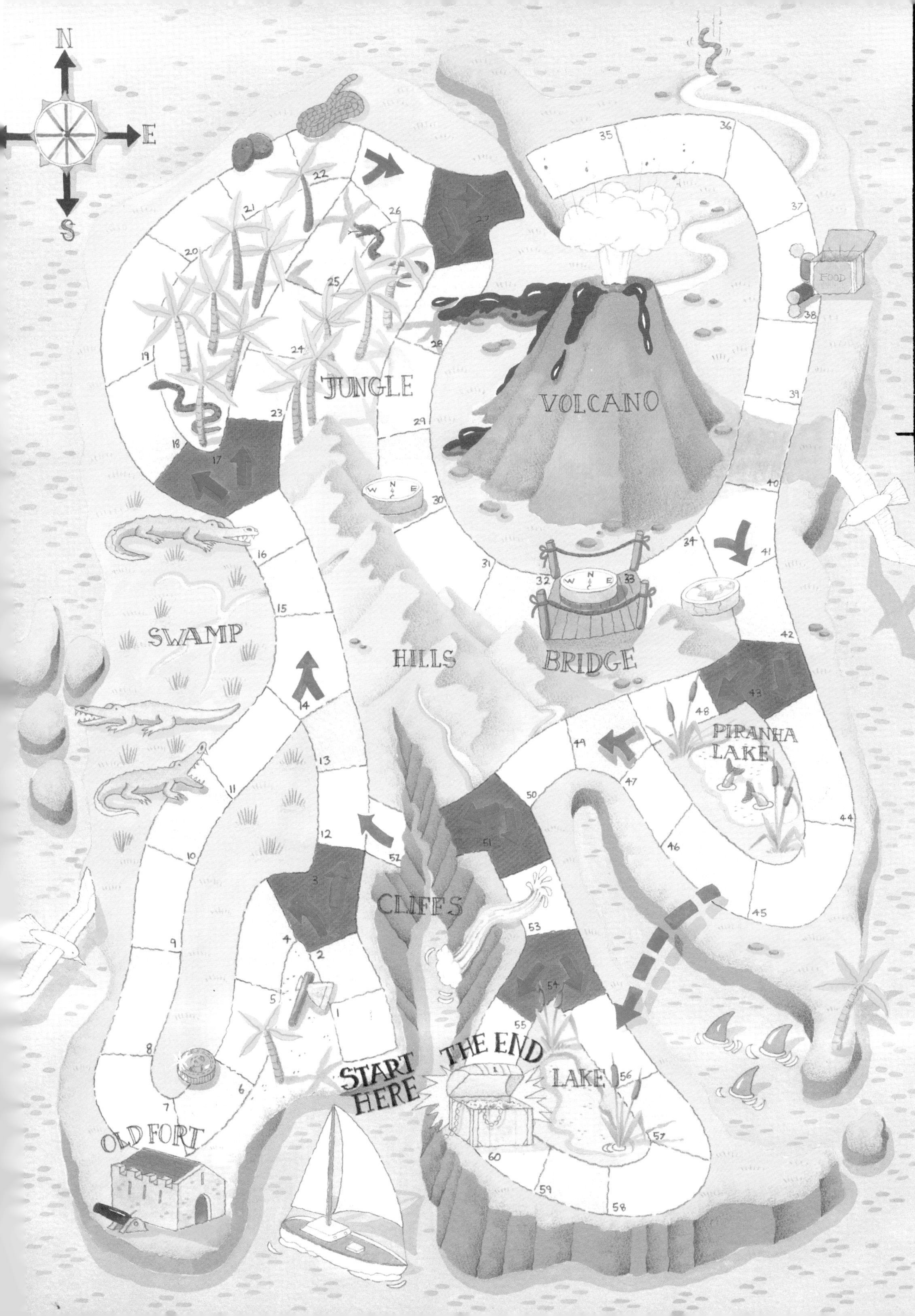

N
E
S
JUNGLE
VOLCANO
FOOD
SWAMP
HILLS
BRIDGE
PIRANHA LAKE
CLIFFS
START HERE
THE END
LAKE
OLD FORT

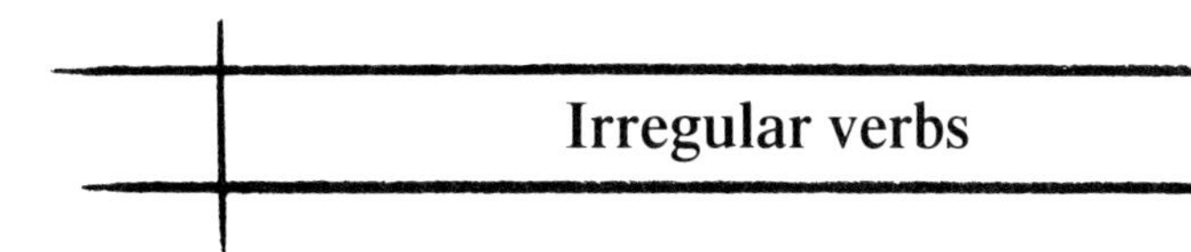

Irregular verbs

Infinitive	Past tense	Infinitive	Past tense	Infinitive	Past tense	Infinitive	Past tense
be	was/were	feel	felt	light	lit	sit	sat
beat	beat	fight	fought	lose	lost	sleep	slept
become	became	find	found	make	made	speak	spoke
begin	began	fly	flew	mean	meant	spend	spent
bite	bit	forget	forgot	meet	met	stand	stood
break	broke	get	got	pay	paid	steal	stole
bring	brought	give	gave	put	put	swim	swam
build	built	go	went	read	read	take	took
buy	bought	grow	grew	ride	rode	teach	taught
catch	caught	have	had	ring	rang	tear	tore
choose	chose	hear	heard	run	ran	tell	told
come	came	hide	hid	say	said	think	thought
cost	cost	hit	hit	see	saw	throw	threw
cut	cut	hurt	hurt	sell	sold	wake	woke
do	did	keep	kept	send	sent	wear	wore
drink	drank	know	knew	shine	shone	win	won
drive	drove	learn	learnt	shoot	shot	write	wrote
eat	ate	leave	left	shut	shut		
fall	fell	lend	lent	sing	sang		

Listening appendix

Unit two

 **Four conversations**

Conversation 1

A Hi.
B Good morning.
A Yeah ... er ... give me an egg salad, please, and ... um ... an apple pie.
B An egg salad and an apple pie. Anything to drink?
A Yeah ... give me an orange juice, please.
B Right.

Conversation 2

A 'Afternoon.
B Good afternoon. Can I help you?
A Yes, please. A tuna sandwich, please ... and ... er ... a chicken sandwich.
B OK. Anything else?
A Mmmm. A drink ... a tea, please. Oh, and an ice cream.
B Fine. That's three pounds fourteen.
A Here you are.
B Thank you. Goodbye.

Conversation 3

A Good evening. A cheese salad, an apple juice ... and an apple pie, please.
B OK. Is that all?
A Yes, that's all. Thank you very much.
B Fine. You can pay over there.

Conversation 4

A Hi.
B Hi.
A A chicken salad and an egg sandwich, please.
B Anything for dessert?
A Oh, yes. Um ... an apple ... no, an ice cream, please.
B An ice cream. Drink?
A An ... no. No, thank you. That's fine.

Unit four

 **Three people**

1 Hi, I'm Gary Taylor. That's T–A–Y–L–O–R. I'm a midfield player for Liverpool and England. I'm from Liverpool, and my address is 95 Kennedy Road, Liverpool. OK? 95 Kennedy Road. And my phone number? Oh, that's 051–447–6322.

2 Good morning. My name's Wilson ... Lisa Wilson ... and my address? Yes, it's 161 Snowdon Road ... Snowdon? That's S–N–O–W–D–O–N, Snowdon road, Southampton. Spell Southampton? Oh, all right ... it's S–O–U–T–H–A–M–P–T–O–N. And my phone number? Yes, it's 0703–88664. OK? Yes. I can wait.

3 Hello, I'm Sarah Jones. I'm a student, and I live in London. Where? Oh, I live at number 108, Cambridge Road – that's C–A–M–B–R–I–D–G–E, London SE13. My phone number? Oh, there isn't a telephone in the house.

Unit six

 **Announcements**

1 The twenty forty train to London is now leaving from platform four.

2 The twenty-one hundred train to Oxford, calling at Basingstoke and Reading, is at platform two.

3 The twenty-one fifteen departure to Bournemouth is now standing at platform three. Passengers for Brockenhurst take the first three carriages.

4 Passengers for the twenty-one fifty train to Manchester and Liverpool please go at once to platform four.

5 The twenty-two thirty to Portsmouth is now arriving at platform one.

Unit nine

 **Women's 200-metre race**

Announcer Well, here we are at the start of the women's two hundred metres.

Starter Ready? On your marks ... get set ...

Announcer They're off. And the Australian's in front. She's very fast ... very fast. The British girl and the Chinese are behind her, and the Spanish girl and the Dutch runner are behind them. Now the German girl is next to the Dutch girl ... oh, she's in front of her. The British girl's in front of the Chinese, yes ... she's just behind the Australian. Oh, look at that! It's the Spanish runner, she's next to the Chinese, now she's in front of her ... Fifty metres to go ... and it's the Spanish girl in front, then the Australian ... the Chinese is behind the British girl, then the German ... and the Dutch girl's behind her ... and that's it!

And here's the result. The Spanish girl is the winner, the Australian is second, the British is third, the Chinese runner is fourth, the German runner is fifth, and the Dutch girl is sixth.

Unit eleven

 **What's in the fridge?**

Man Is there any food in the fridge, Janet? I'm really hungry ...
Woman Well, there's some butter, some fruit. And there are some tomatoes.
Man Is that all? Isn't there any meat, or eggs, or anything?
Woman Well, there *are* some eggs, but they're very old. There isn't any chicken left ... or any salad ... and there aren't any hamburgers.
Man What about in the door?
Woman There's some cheese. Ergh! That's very old, too. And some milk. The milk's OK. Oh, and a bottle of Perrier water, well, half a bottle.
Man Oh, well. Let's go to a restaurant, then ...

Unit thirteen

(c) Who are they talking about?

1 How old? I don't know . . . about twenty-five or twenty-six, I think. He's average-build. He's got dark hair . . . dark-brown hair, and he's got a beard. He's wearing a short-sleeved shirt. It's kind of green, with . . . well, he's wearing bluish trousers. Light-blue trousers.

2 What's she like? Er . . . she's good-looking. She isn't tall. She's average-height, I'd say. She's got nice hair. It's blond, and quite short, really. I suppose she's about 35 or 36. She's wearing a brown suit, it's got a nice jacket.

3 What's he like? Umm . . . he's average-height, in his twenties, I think. He's got brown hair, it's not very long. He's quite good-looking. He looks very fit . . . well, he *is* a sportsman. He's wearing a pullover and trousers, there are a lot of colours in the pullover. I don't like it very much.

Unit sixteen

Seaville

1 Now, let me think . . . yes, go along this street to the end, then go across the river. Turn right and walk along River Street . . . about eight hundred metres. The castle's at the end of the street. You can't miss it.

2 Yes . . . well, take the first right, go past the supermarket and turn left at the end of the road. Then take the first road on the right. It's called . . . er, West Road, I think. You'll see it on your right. It isn't very far. Don't go past it!

3 Ah . . . I'm a stranger here myself, actually. But I think I know. Go along this street, go straight past the cathedral . . . you can't miss the cathedral, and go straight on to the river. Go across the bridge, and turn . . . turn right. Go past the railway station, it's on the left, and carry straight on to the next road on the left. Turn left, and walk along that street. Go over the railway bridge, and it's on your left. It's a long way!

4 You're going the wrong way. Turn round and go along Cathedral Street to Sea Road. Turn left and go straight on to the sea. Turn right at the Promenade . . . and it's the second hotel on right. You can't miss it.

Unit twenty

Dinner

1 **Waiter** Good evening, madam.
Woman Good evening. Could I have the menu, please?
Waiter Certainly, madam. Here it is.
Woman Thank you. What's the soup of the day?
Waiter Chicken.
Woman Fine. A chicken soup, please. And fish and chips.
Waiter Would you like a dessert?
Woman Yes, please. I'd like a fruit salad.

2 **Waiter** Good evening, sir. What would you like?
Man I'd like melon with ham for a starter.
Waiter And the main course?
Man Could I have a steak, please?
Waiter How would you like it?
Man Well-done, please. And could I have a side salad?
Waiter Anything else, sir?
Man Yes, an ice cream, please.
Waiter What flavour would you like?
Man Vanilla, please.

3 **Woman** Could we see the menu, please?
Waiter Yes. Here you are, madam.
Woman Could we have two tomato soups?
Waiter Yes, madam. Anything else?
Woman Yes, we'd like two chicken, please.
Waiter Anything for dessert?
Woman Have you got a fruit salad?
Waiter Yes, madam.
Woman Fine. One fruit salad, and one strawberry ice cream, please.

Unit twenty-two

Three conversations

1 **A** Four, please.
B Which film?
A Oh, sorry . . . for Rumba 5.
B That's £14.
A What time's the next performance?
B It's at twenty past five.
A Thank you.

2 **C** Could I have six tickets for The Yorkshire Ballet, please?
D Which day?
C For Thursday, please.
D Where would you like to sit?
C At the front, please.
D We haven't got six seats at the front . . . what about the middle?
C Right . . . that's fine.

3 **E** Hello?
F Cannon Cinemas . . . Can I help you?
E Er . . . yes, what time's *The Mountain of the Giants*?
F The first performance is at five to two, madam.
E Oh dear. That's too early. What time's the next performance?
F Five past three.
E That's OK. How much are the tickets?
F They're three fifty.
E Thank you.

Unit twenty-five

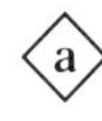

What's happening?

Cobb It's going to stop . . . Yes, it's stopping outside number 20. A man's getting out. Look at that! It's Willy Craig, the bank robber. Come on, are you taking photographs or not?
Kennedy Great! He's going in. He's ringing the door bell.
Cobb The door's opening. I can see Butcher Bailey. Butcher Bailey and Willy Craig. What's happening?
Kennedy They're walking to the car. I can't see the driver . . .
Cobb I can . . . it's Kevin Daniels.
Kennedy They're getting into the car . . . Come on, hurry!

Unit twenty-nine

c **Four jobs**

1 Hi, my name's Gary ... Gary Miller, and I live in Manchester. Do I work regular hours? Well, I never work on Mondays. I work from ten to one every day. Sometimes I work on Wednesday evenings ... or Tuesday evenings. I always work on Saturdays. Oh, but I don't work in the summer. Now, what do I do? I'm a footballer ... I play for Manchester United!

2 In the police we work shifts. This month I'm on the early shift, and I begin at 6 a.m. and work until 2 p.m. Sometimes I'm on the late shift, and then I always work from 2 p.m. until 10 p.m. I don't like the night shift. I'm going to be on that next month. The night shift begins at 10 p.m. and finishes at six in the morning. Does my job have regular hours? Well, I don't know, really. I work the same hours every day for a month. But my days off are different every month: this month they're Thursday and Sunday.

3 I start work at five, or half past five in the morning. I'm a farmer. We've got a small farm in the west of England. We stop and have breakfast at eight. We work all day. We finish at six or seven in the evening ... sometimes later. Do we have days off? No, we don't! We work seven days a week. The animals never have Sundays off, and we can't! We always work Sunday mornings from six to eight, and again in the afternoon from four to six. We've got sixty cows, and we need to milk them.

I work at home. I'm a computer programmer. I go into the company's office once or twice a week for meetings, but I do all my work in my office at home. It's easy, really. I've got a computer here, a modem – that's a telephone link between my computer and the company's computer – and a telefax machine. I work about thirty-five hours a week. Sometimes I work twelve hours a day, and some days I only work two or three hours. I never work on Saturdays and Sundays. I always get the children from school at four o'clock, and I never work between four and six. In the future I think there are going to be more jobs like mine.

Unit thirty-one

Snacks survey

Man 071–115–9872.
Julie Good afternoon. I'm doing a market research survey. Could I ask you some questions, please?
Man Well, I'm busy, but I suppose so ...
Julie Thank you. Right ... How often do you eat between meals?
Man Are you serious? Oh, I don't know ... quite often, really. I mean, every day.
Julie That's fine. And do you eat any of these things? I'm going to read a list. OK?
Man OK.
Julie Fruit?
Man No.
Julie Nuts?
Man No, never.
Julie Crisps?
Man Yes, sometimes.
Julie Biscuits?
Man Uh huh.
Julie Sorry?
Man Yes.
Julie And chocolate?
Man No, hardly ever.
Julie And when do you usually have snacks? I mean, what time of day?
Man Well, in the mornings, and the afternoons ... and when I'm watching TV.
Julie And where do you eat snacks?
Man That's a silly question. At home, in the office ...
Julie In the street?
Man No, never. Are there any more questions?
Julie No many. How often do you *buy* snacks?
Man Er ... every day. Well, nearly every day.
Julie And which of these makes of chocolate do you know? There's another list, I'm afraid.
Man Go on.
Julie Nestlé?
Man Yes.
Julie Suchard?
Man Yes.
Julie Hershey?
Man No. Never heard of it.
Julie Cadbury?
Man Yes.
Julie Mars?
Man Yes.
Julie Chockie Bar?
Man What?
Julie Chockie Bar.
Man Oh, yes. There's an advert on TV. Yes, I know it.
Julie Last question ...
Man Good.
Julie Would you like a free Chockie Bar? We can send you one by post ...
Man No. Um, ooh, yes, yes, I would. Thanks.
Julie Good. I know you're going to like it.
Man I'm not going to eat it. I don't want it. But my dog loves chocolate ...

Unit thirty-six

Regular verbs: sounds
The listening exercise uses the text in Unit thirty-six.

Unit thirty-seven

Which is the friendly conversation?

1 **Conversation A**
■ It's a nice day, isn't it?
□ Yes, it is.

Conversation B
■ It's a nice day, isn't it?
□ Yes, it is.

2 **Conversation A**
■ Did you see that programme about Australia last night?
□ Oh, no, I didn't. Was it good?

Conversation B
■ Did you see *Quiz of the Week* on TV yesterday?
□ No, I never watch quiz shows.

3 **Conversation A**
■ Here you are. That's three pounds.
□ Thank you.

Conversation B
■ There you are. That's two pounds.
□ Thank you very much.

4 **Conversation A**

■ Can I help you?
□ Yes, thank you. I'd like some information . . .

Conversation B

■ Can I help you?
□ Hello. Yes, I want some information . . .

5 **Conversation A**

■ Do you often come here?
□ No, hardly ever. It's very nice, isn't it?

Conversation B

■ Do you often come here?
□ Yes, I do. I work here!

6 **Conversation A**

■ Do you speak English?
□ Yes. Why?

Conversation B

■ Can you speak English?
□ Well, yes . . . a little.

Unit thirty-eight

You'll finish soon?

1 I'll leave at 6 o'clock.
2 We'll arrive at 7.
3 They play football.
4 I'll have a bath at 8 o'clock.
5 You finish soon.
6 He'll put it there.

Vocabulary index

Note: P = passive vocabulary C = classroom vocabulary
eg: look-C1, 3 means the word is classroom vocabulary in Unit 1, and taught actively in Unit 3.

a-2
abbreviation-C19
abilities-P21
about-C4, 13
above-7
accepting-P39
actor-29
act out-C39
across-16
actress-P13
A.D.-36
add-C36
address-4
adult-17
adventure-P37
advertisement-P21
aerobics-P37
aeroplane-3
afraid-24
Africa-19
afternoon-2
again-25
against-36
age-7
agent-27
agreeing-P39
agriculture-P18
ahead of (time)-24
air-P19
airline-29
airmail-19
airport-P5, 11
album-P19
algebra-P21
alive-P13, 39
all-13
all right-23
along-16
alphabet-4
also-21
altogether-14
always-29
am ('m)-1
a.m.-P2, 24
amazing-24
ambassador-P13
ambulance-P35
America-P4, 19
American-7
an-2
ancestor-P36
anchovies-P11
and-C1, 2
angry-37
animal-21
announcement-C6
another-C7, P21
answer (v)-C4, 27
answer (n)-C7
antibiotic-P11
any-10
anybody-25
any more-28
anyone-35
anything-21
anything else-2
anyway-28
anywhere-39
apple-2
April-24
are ('re)-1
area-P31
arm-P39
armour-P36
around-31
arrive-P33, 36
arrow-P40
Asia-19
ask-C4, P16, 27
asleep-17
aspirin-34
astronomer-7
at-C1, 3, 22
at all-37
athletics-P37
atlas-P16
attendant-23
August-24
aunt-12
Australasia-19
Australia-1
Australian-9
author-P24
automatic-P23
autumn-37
avenue-16
average-13
away from-24
awful-37
axe-P40
baby-18
back-15
bad-11
badge-C7, P14
bag-5
baker-34
balcony-P13
ballet-22
banana-14
band-P22
bank-16
bass-P21
bath-34
bathroom-17
battery-19
B.C.-36
be-15
beach-39
beard-13
beautiful-8
because-28
bed-28
bedroom-17
beef-34
beer-18
before-32
beg-P17
begin-29
behind-9
behind (time)
below-P8, 9
belt-P17
best seller-P27
Best wishes-5
between-C3, P31, 36
beware-33
big-8
bike-P27
bingo-P3
bird-24
birthday-38
biscuit-11
black-8
blind-21
blond-13
blouse-13
blue-8
board-C6
boat-8
body-17
Bolognese-P20
book-3
bookcase-28
borrow-32
both-36
bottle-19
bought-34
bowl-11
box-C2, 15
boxer-P13, 29
box office-P22
boy-15
brakes-P39
branch-34
Brazil-1
Brazilian-7
bread-11
breakfast-11
bridge-16
briefcase-5
bright-24
British-7
broken-39
brother-12
brown-8
buffet-P6
build (of body)-13
burglar-P37
bus-3
business-P25
businessman-12
bus stop-16
busy-20
but-21
butter-11
buy-P31, 34
by-17
cactus-P28
cake-18
calculator-8
calendar-38
call-32
called (to be)-31
camera-C10, 14
can (v)-P14, 21
can't-P16, 21
cap-19
capital-10
Captain-23
car-3
card (post)-P19
cardigan-P17
careful-15
carefully-P35
careless-33
car park-P6, 16
carpet-28
carry-39
cartoon-P22
case-30
cassette-3
cassette player-3
castle-16
cat-12
cathedral-P16
CD-P28
Celsius (°C)-26
centre-P16
chauffeur-P13
chair-C6, 15
champagne-P27
championship-P4
change (v)-30
chart-C4
cheese-2
cheeseburger-2
cheetah-P21
chemist-34
cheque-34
cherry-14
chewing-gum-P35
chicken-2
child-12
children-12
chilli-P11
Chinese-7
chips-20
chocolate-14
choose-40
chorus-C13
Christmas-P27
church-16
cinema-22
city-24
class (n)-C9
class (1st class)-19
classical-22
clean-11
cleaner-P13, 37
clear-24
cloak-P35
clock-10
close (v)-C3, 15
closed-17
clothes-27
cloud-C26
cloudy-26
clown-P13
class-9
classroom-C5
clean (v)-30
cliff-P40
cloakroom-17
coat-33
coffee-1
coffee pot-10
coin-40
cola-2
cold-C23, 26
collect-37
college-P28
colour-8
come-4
comedy-37
come on-5
comet-P24
compact disc-19
company-21
compass-P40
competition-8
complete-C5
computer-3
concert-22
contestant-10
continue-C5, 37
control-P25
conversation-C1, 37
cooker-8
cool-26
co-pilot-P9, 23
corner-35
cornflakes-P11, 30
correct-10
corridor-35
could (request)-20
Count-P35
cousin-12
countable-C11
counter-P40
country-7
cow-C29
crazy-P13
credit card-P33
crew-7
crewman-9
criminal-5
crisps-P31
cross (x)-C11
cross (v)-39
crossing-P33
cup-3
cupboard-28
curly-13
curtains-28
customs-5
customs officer-P5
cut-P8
Czechoslovakia-P4
'd (would)-19
daily-P22
dance-21
dark-13
dark (blue)-19
darling-20
daughter-12
day-P20, 22
dead-17
Dear ...-5
dear-10
December-24
defender-P4
degree (°)-26
dentist-P30
depart-P33
departures-P6
departure lounge-P33
deputy-P36
describe-C8
desert-P24

desk-28
dessert-P2, 20
destination-P6, 38
detective-5
diamond-5
dice-40
dictionary-3
did(n't)-34
die-36
different-C17, 29
difficult-33
dining room-17
dinner-23
diploma-P28
directions-16
director-29
disabled-21
disagreeing-P39
disc (film)-P14
disco-C5, P16, 39
discover-36
dislike-27
dive-P21
division-P25
do-15, 21
doctor-7
does(n't)-27
dog-9
doing-23
doll-P14
dollar-27
don't-15
don't know-3
door-6
doorbell-C25
double-4
down-9
downstairs-17
drama-P37
draw-C9
drawer-32
dress-13
dressing room-P4
drink (v, n)-23
drink (n)-2
drive (v)-21
driver-6
driving-P18
drown-36
drummer-21
drums-21
dry-26
Dutch-8
each-14
early-5
Earth-P1, 7
earth (soil)-28
east-19
eastern-31
Easter-26
eat-23
egg-2
eighth-8
electricity-11
elephant-P39
emergency-31
empty-32
encyclopaedia-P18
end-16
engine-3
engineer-7
England-1
English-8
enjoy-37
entrance-6
envelope-28
Europe-19
European-29
evening-2
every-29
every day-29
everything-P20, 23
exact-40
example-C29
exciting-25
Excuse me-6
exercise-C11
exit-P1, 16
expensive-8
exposure-P14
eye-13
face-33
factory-12
falcon-P21
fall (v)-36
fall (n) (US = autumn)-P10
false-C11
family-12
famous-12
fantastic-4
far-21
farm-C29, 31
farmer-C29
farming-31
fast-8
fasten-P1
fat-13
father-12
favourite-12
February-24
fell-36
fever-P39
few-34
fifth-8
film (for camera)-14
film (movie)-27
finally-36
find-C7, 35
find out-C34
fine-2
finish-29
fire (v)-36
first-4
fish-20
fishing-P18
flag-8
flat (n)-12
flavour-14
flight-23
floor-18, 28
fly (v)-P21, 23
fog-37
foggy-37
fold-P40
folk (music)-P37
follow-17
food-11
foot (on foot)-31
football-4
for (price)-P8
for (time)-C3, 29
for (him/her etc.)-14
forecast-P26, 37
forecaster-C26
forget-P39
fork-3
form (order)-C11
form (competition)-P8
fortnight-P27
found-35
fourth-8
France-1
free (vacant)-6
free-31
French-7
Friday-22
fridge-8
friend-12
friendly-9
frighten-35
frightened-35
from-1
front-22
fruit-11
funny-35
future-C38
game-C3
garden-15
gas-11
gate (airport)-38
gentlemen-10
German-8
Germany-8
get-5
get into-C25
get married-38
get out of-C25, 30
giant-P22
girl-6
give-C15, 32
glass-3
glasses-13
go-4
goal-36
goalkeeper-P4
go away-26
going to do-25
gold-10
golf club-P10
good-12
goodbye-2
good-looking-13
Good morning-2
goodness (Thank)-P38
go out-29
got ('ve got)-12
got-34
governor-P36
gram-19
grandchild-12
granddaughter-12
grandfather-12
grandmother-12
grandparent-12
grandson-12
grape-14
great!-34
Great Britain-P3
greatest-P19
Greece-1
Greek-10
green-8
grey-8
groan-C35
ground (floor)-28
group-C15, 21
guard-P6
guess-C21, 29
guest-P5
guest registration card-C5
guide-17
guitar-21
guitarist-21
gun-25
had-34
hair-P8, 13
hair dryer-8
half-14
hall-15
Halloween-P35
hamburger-2
hand-5
handbag-18
handle-15
happen-24
happy-5
hardly ever-31
has-12
hat-27
have (got)-12
have-C5, 24
he-1
headache-39
hear-21
heard-35
heart-P39
heavy-18
height-13
helicopter-9
hello-1
help (v)-P14, 15
her-4, 9
here-4
Here you are-2
hers-18
Hi-5
hi-fi-21
high-24
hill-24
him-9
his-4, 18
hit (record)-P19
hit (v)-23
hobbies-P37
hold-15
holiday-26
Holland-8
home-7
home town-7
horrible-35
horror-37
horse-36
hospital-11
hot-11
hot dog-2
hotel-C5, 16
hour-P3, 19
hours (regular hours)-19
house-12
hovercraft-P33
How are you?-1
How many?-17
How much? (price)-6
How often?-31
How old?-7
huge-24
hundred-6
hungry-28
hurry-20
husband-12
I-1
ice-24
ice cream-2
ice lolly-14
idea-39
identikit-P33
identity card-5
independence-P21, P38
if-P17
important-37
impossible-33
in-C2, 5
India-19
information-6
in front of-9
inland-P19
inside-15
inspector-P5, 33
instructions-C15
instrument-21
interested-37
interests-P37
international-P4, 7
interview (n)-27
interview (v)-C7
into-25
irregular-29
Ireland-29
Irish-29
is ('s)-1
island-3
it-3, 9
Italy-1
Italian-8
jacket-13
January-24
jam-P14
Japan-1
Japanese-7
jazz-P18, 22
jeans-8
jigsaw-C34
job-7
joke-37
judo-P37
jug-11
juice-2
July-24
jump-P21
June-24
jungle-P40
just-P13, 28
kangaroo-P18
key-3
keyboard-21
kids-17
kill-35
kilogram-36
kilometre-P3, 7
kind (nice)-18
kind (type)-29
kiosk-P6
king-36
kiss (n, v)-P27, 30
kitchen-P8
knife-3
know-3, 5
laboratory-34
ladder-15
ladies-10
Lady-17
lake-P40
land (v)-36
landing-17
language-10
large-14
last-22, 23
late-5
laugh-35
leave (v)-30
left (opp. right)-16
left (past leave)-38
left luggage-P6
lemon-11
let's-34
letter (post)-8
letter (ABC)-C13
licence-P21
life-30
lift-28
light (n)-24
light (blue)-19
lighthouse-P16
like (description)-8
like ('d like)-19
like (v)-27
liquid-P34
list-C10, 34
listen-C1, 3
litre-35
little-15
live (v)-29
lives (pl. n)-29

living room-17
'll (will)-38
local-P33
lock-15
locked-15
lonely-P35
long-P3, 13
look-C1, 3
Lord-17
lost-4
lot (a lot of)-26
lotion-P19
loud-39
love (v)-P10, 28
lovely-13
low-39
L.P.-19
lunch-11
lunch-time-20
'm (am)-1
mad-P39
madam-C20
magazine-8
main-31
main course-20
make (v)-C6, 30
make (n)-8
make up-P28, 35
man-3
manager-P21
many-17
map-16
March-24
market research-P31
market researcher-P31
marmalade-P14
married-12
marry (v)-36
Mars-P1
match (v)-C4
matter (What's the matter?)-35
May-24
me-P6, 9
meal-31
mean (v)-C34
meat-11
medicine-11
medium-14
meet-P12
melon-P20
member-C7
menu-20
metre-9
midfield-P4
middle-22
middle-aged-13
Middle East-19
midnight-24
mile-17
milk-11
millimetre-14
million-27
mine-18
minestrone-20
minus-C24
minute-C3, 19
mirror-28
Miss-13
miss (v) (you can't miss it)-P16, 38
mistake-36
mix up-P40
model-P8, P12
moment-23
Monday-22
money-12
monster-P16
month-24
more-C3
morning-2
mosquito-P31
mother-12
motor cycle-C23
motor bike-31
mountain-P22
moustache-13
move-15
movie-39
Mr-13
Mrs-13
Ms-27
multinational-P21
mum(my)-15
mushroom-P11
music-27
musical-21
musician-21
my-24
'n' (and)-28
name-4
national-P38
nationality-7
navigator-P36
near-24
need-28
neighbour-37
nephew-12
never-29
new-7
news-P6, 11
newsreader-P13
New Zealand-P21
next-6
next (week etc.)-26
next to-6
nice-P13, 25
niece-12
night-2
no-1
no (not any)-P13
noise-23
noon-24
north-19
northern-31
note (money)-18
note-C6
notebook-C11, 14
nothing-25
nought-C14
novel-P12
November-24
now-4
no way!-P27
number-C2, 3
number (v)-P8
nurse-P11, 29
nuts-P31
obey-P40
object (n)-40
occupation-P5, 31
o'clock-5
October-24
of-C7, 10
of course-32
off (the menu)-20
offer-C28, 39
office-6
officer-29
often-31
Oh dear!-4
oil rig-P29
OK-2
old-8
olives-P11
on-5
on (Thursday etc.)-22
one (this one)-16
onion-11
only-17
open (adj.)-3
open (v)-C3, 10
operation-P33
or-26
orange (n)-2
orange (adj)-13
orchestra-3
order (1, 2, 3)-C11
order (command)-C15
order (a meal)-P20
other-C4, 15
our-5
ours-18
outback-P31
outside-C15, 25
overseas-P19
over-23
over (more than)-31
over there-3
owe-32
owl-C35
painting (n)-17
pair-19
pale (blue etc.)-P13
paper-15
paragraph-C34
Pardon?-2
parents-12
part-C25
partner-C4
party-13
passenger-23
passport-P5, 33
past (go past)-16
past (clock)-22
past (tense)-C32
pay-32
pear-14
peas-P20
pen-3
pence (p)-2
pencil-14
penguin-P24
people-C4, 13
pepper-P11
perfect-P11
per cent (%)-P20
performance-22
per hour-P3
period-P33
Persian (carpet)-P37
person-12
personal-P8
pet-12
phone (n)-4
phone (v)-24
photograph-P5, 24
physics-P18
piano-21
pickpocket-33
picture-C1, 3
pie-2
pilot-7
pineapple-P11, 14
pink-8
pirate-P36
piranha-P40
pizza-2
place-24
plan-C9, P16
plane-5
plant-28
plate-3
platform-6
play-21
player-4, 21
PLC (= Public Limited Company)-P21
please-1
pleased-17
plus-C24
p.m.-24
P.O. Box-P8
point (.)-C14
poison(-ing)-34
police-3
policeman-C4
policewoman-C4
polite-C15
politician-P13
poor (Tracey)!-32
pop (music)-27
population-31
port-33
Portugal-26
postcard-14
poster-28
post-31
postman-15
post office-16
pot-10
potato-11
pound (£)-2
pound (lb.)-14
president-29
price-P22
priest-29
prisoner-15
private-17
prize-8
problem-38
programme-C4, P12, 15
programmer-C29
public-P16, 17
public health department-34
pull-9
pullover-13
purse-15
push-15
put-C2, 9
put (past)-35
put on (clothes)-30
quarter-14
question-10
questionnaire-P12, 31
quick-25
quiet-15
quiz-10
race-9
racing driver-P13
racket-P10, 28
radio-3
railway-6
rain (v, n)-26
rank (taxis)-P16
rare (meat)-20
're (are)-1
read-C2, 21
reading-C22, 27
refusing-P39
Really?-13
reception-35
receptionist-P5
record (n)-13
recorder-8
red-8
referee-C4
registration-P5
regular-29
religious-P38
remember-33
repeat-C1
report-P11, 24
reporter-P7, 11
representative-P21
request-C15
rescue-P9
return (n)-6
rice-27
rich-12
ride-31
Right-5
right (correct)-10
right (opp. left)-16
ring-C25
river-36
rob (v)-25
robber (n)-25
robbery (n)-25
rock-9
rock (music)-P12, 22
role play-C5
rolls-P34
romantic-P12, 36
room-5
rope-40
round (shape)-C33
round (direction)-35
rule-C36, 40
ruler-14
run-21
runner-9
Russian-7
's (is)-1
's (has)-12
's (possession)-12
said-35
sail (v)-36
salad-2
salami-P11
sales-P21
same-29
sandwich-1
Saturday-22
sauce-P11
sausage-20
saw-35
saxophone-21
say-C4, 35
scales-P19
scar-C33
school-28
science fiction-37
scientist-7
score (v)-36
Scotland-1
sea-9
seaside-P39
seat-6
seat belts
seaport-P33
second (2nd)-5
second (n) (time)-10
secretary-29
see-21
self-service-P2
sell-P21
semi-final-P4
send-P8, 34
sentences-C12
September-24
sergeant-P25
series-P12, 27
serve (v)-23
service-P20
seventh-8
sex-P31
shall-39

shave-30
she-1
sheep-31
shelf-28
sheriff-P36
shift-29
shine-26
shirt-8
shoe-C8, 13
shop-C11, P19, 34
shopping (n)-27
short-13
show (n)-39
shower-30
shown-P33
shut up-27
side-22
sideburns-C33
silly-35
silver-10
sing-21
singer-10
single-6
sir-20
sister-12
sit-15
sixth-8
size-14
skirt-13
sky-24
sleep (v)-23
sleep (n)-25
slip (v)-36
slow-8
small-8
smile (v)-37
snack-31
snow (v, n)-26
soap opera-P27
socks-C18
soft-P39
some-10
someone-35
something-35
sometimes-29
somewhere-39
son-12
song-C1, 21
soon-38
sorry-4
soul (music)-P27
sound (v)-37
soup-20
south-19
southern-31
souvenir-14
space (gap)-C13, 39
space-7
space station-7
spaghetti-20
Spain-1
Spanish-7
speak-21
speaker-3
specialist-7
spell-4
spend (money)-26
spinner-P40
spoon-3
sport-12
sports-P8
sportsperson-12
spring-37
springtime-P10
square (km)-P31
square-C33
St. (saint)-P38
stadium-P16
stage-22
stairs-17
stamp-19
stand (v)-10
star-P1, 3
start (v)-25
starter (meal)-20
starting time-P29
state-31
station-6
stay (v)-26
steak-20
stereo-P8
sticker-P19
stop (v)-23
store (shop)-P28
story-27
straight on-16
stranger-16
strawberry-14
street-16
striker-P4
student-C3, 5
stupid-35
success-P27
sugar-11
suggestion-39
suit-13
suitcase-5
summer-26
sun-26
Sunday-26
sunglasses-18
sunlight-P28
sunny-26
sun tan-P19
supermarket-16
sure-32
surface (mail)-P19
surname-4
surprised-37
survey-31
swamp-P40
swan-P21
Sweden-8
Swedish-8
swim-21
swimming (n)-27
symphony-P22
synthesizer-21
table-C6, 10
take-16
take (photos)-24
talk-C4, 24
talk about-C8
tall-13
taxi-6
tea-2
tea (meal)-11
teacher-C1, 29
teeth-30
telephone-P4, 10
telephone box-16
telephone number-4
television-3
tell-C12, 16
temperature-26
tennis-4
terrible-13
thanks-2
thank you-1
that-P3, 6
That's (£1/£2 etc.)-2
the-1
theatre-39
their-5
theirs-18
them-9
then (in that case)-28
then (time)-30
there (opp. here)-6
there (is / are)-10
these-6
they-3, 5
thin-13
thing-C10, 11
think-C7, 24
third-8
thirsty-28
this-6
this way-4
those-6
thousand-7
threw-C40
through-15
throw (n, v)-40
throw away-28
thunder (n, v)-26
Thursday-22
tick-C2 (√)
ticket-6
tidy (adj, v)-28
tie (n)-13
time-5
timer-P35
times (six times)-31
timetable-33
tired-39
title-P5
to-4
to (clock)-22
together-32
toilets-6
tomato-11
tomorrow-26
tonight-P10, 24
too (also)-5
too (big etc)-39
took-37
toothbrush-35
toothpaste-P34
towards-24
towel-35
town-7
traffic-39
train-6
trainers (shoes)-C18, 28
translate-21
translator-21
transparent-C18
travel-24
traveller-33
treasure-P40
tree-35
trousers-13
Trouser-suit-13
truck-8
true-5
trumpet-21
T-shirt-13
Tuesday-22
tuna-2
Turkish-8
Turkey-8
turn (v)-16
turn (n)-40
turn off-15
turn on-15
two-way-P31
type (v)-21
type (kind)-P21
typewriter-10
typist-32
umbrella-3
uncle-12
uncountable-C11
under-9
underline-C34
unhappy-38
United Nations-P21
United States-1
untidy-C28
until-29
up-9
upstairs-30
us-9
usually-30
use (v)-24
valuable-37
vampire-C35
vanilla-14
V.A.T.-P20
vehicle-P3
've (have)-1
verb-C36
very-P2, 13
very well-2
video-3
video cassette-19
villa-P12
visit (n)-27
volcano-P11
volleyball-P27
volt-P39
volume-P18
wait-15
waiter-20
waiting room-P6
wake-25
wake up-30
walk-21
Walkman™-P8, 19
wall-17
want-28
want to do-36
war-37
wardrobe-28
warm-26
wash (n)-34
washing up-P34
was(n't)-32
waste bin-28
watch (n)-3
watch (v)-C23, 26
water-9
way-16
we-5
wear-13
weather-26
wedding-36
Wednesday-22
week-P10, 22
weekend-P8, 31
weigh (v)-36
welcome-10
well (adj)-2
well (hesitation)-6
well done (meat)-20
went-34
were(n't)-32
west-19
western (adj)-31
western (film)-37
wet-26
whale-21
What?-3
What about?-20
What time?-6
wheelchair-21
When?-22
Where?-1, 5
where (relative)-P39
Which?-18
white-8
Who?-7
Whose?-18
Why?-25
wife-12
wild-P31
will-38
win-8
window-C6, P9, 15
wind-C26
windy-26
winner-8
winter-26
with-C8, 13
woman-3
wonderful-10
won't-38
word-C8, 21
work (n, v)-C17, 24
workdays-C29
world-P13, 24
worry-38
would-19
write-C1, 21
writer-12
wrong-20
yeah-3
year-26
yellow-8
yes-1
yesterday-32
yoga-P37
yoghurt-18
you-1, 5, 9
young-13
your-4, 5
yours-18
Yugoslavia-P26
zone-19

Grammar summaries

Unit one

***Be** present singular*
Personal pronouns: ***I, you, he, she***

I	'm am 'm not	
You	're are aren't	Peter Wilson. Sarah Kennedy. from England.
He She	's is isn't	

Questions

Am I		Yes, I am. / No, I'm not.
Are you	Peter Wilson? Sarah Kennedy? from England?	Yes, you are / No, you aren't.
Is he she		Yes, he is. / No, he isn't. Yes, she is. / No, she isn't.

Where	are you am I is he she	from?

Expressions

Coffee?
Yes, please. / No, thank you.
Hello.

How are you?
Yes?

Unit two

Indefinite articles: ***a, an***

a	coffee, tea, sandwich, salad, hamburger, pizza
an	apple pie, egg salad, ice cream, orange juice

***an** is used before vowel sounds, **a** is used before consonant sounds.*

Expressions

Good morning. — Goodbye.
Good afternoon. — Goodbye.
Good evening. — Good night.

I'm very well thanks, and you? / I'm fine.
Anything else?
That's (six) pounds, please.

Here you are.
Thanks.
Pardon?

Unit three

***Be** singular and plural, with things*

a / an

It	's is isn't is not	a pen. an engine.
They	're are aren't are not	pens. engines.

Questions

Is	it	a pen? an engine?	Yes, it is. / No, it isn't.
Are	they	pens? engines?	Yes, they are. / No, they aren't.

What is it? / What are they?

Singular and plurals

pen / pens — watch / watches
key / keys — dictionary / dictionaries

Irregular plurals

knife / knives
man / men — woman / women

Expressions

Look! / Listen!
over there.
I don't know.

It's open. / It's OK.
What's that?
Oh no!

Unit four

Personal information: ***name, address, telephone number***

What	's is	your my his her	name? address? telephone number? phone number? number?

Possessive adjectives, singular

My Your His Her	name	is 's isn't is not	Smith.

Personal pronoun – Possessive adjective

I . . . my
You . . . your
He . . . his
She . . . her

Expressions

He's fantastic.
Come here. / Come this way. / Go to (the dressing room). / Go now.
Sorry. / That's OK.
What? (= pardon?)
I'm lost.
Oh dear.
Spell it.

Unit five

Be *present tense, plural*
Personal pronouns: ***we***, ***you***, ***they***

Affirmative and negative

We You They	're are aren't are not	detectives. early. late. in London.

Questions

Are	we you they	late? criminals? in London?	Yes, we are. No, we aren't.

Possessive adjectives, plural forms

It's	our your	car.
They're	their	cars.

Personal pronoun – Possessive adjective

we . . . our
you . . . your
they . . . their

Where is (it)? / Where are (they)?

What's the time? It's six o'clock / six thirty.
It's in the car. It's in the bag. Hands on the car.

Expressions

Hi.
Yeah. (Yes.)
Right.
Get the (bag).
Put your hands on (the car).
Go and look.
We're early / late.
Dear ______, / Best wishes.
Do you know . . .?

Unit six

Demonstratives: ***this, that, these, those***
This *and* ***these*** *are used for things that are nearer,* ***that*** *and* ***those*** *are used for things that are further away.*

This That	is isn't	the London train.
These Those	are aren't	your bags.

Here – this / these There – that / those

Asking about prices with ***How much?***

How much	is	it? this / that?	One pound fifty. Two pounds seventy.

on platform three / next to the entrance.

Expressions

'Afternoon.
Single or return?
How much?
Excuse me!
Are these (seats) free?
Aren't they?

Unit seven

Questions with ***Who?***

Who	is	he? the pilot? from Paris?
	are	they? the scientists?

Asking about age with ***How old?***

How old	am	I?
	is	he? she? it?
	are	you? they? we?

Asking about jobs and nationality

What	's is	my his her your	job? nationality?
	are	our their your	jobs? nationalities?

I'm twenty-eight. / I'm twenty-eight years old.

Indefinite articles ***a, an*** *and definite article* ***the***

She's a doctor. / She's the doctor on the space station.
He's an engineer. / He's the engineer on Icarus.

Nationalities

American / Russian / Brazilian
British / Spanish
Japanese / Chinese
French

Unit eight

Adjectives

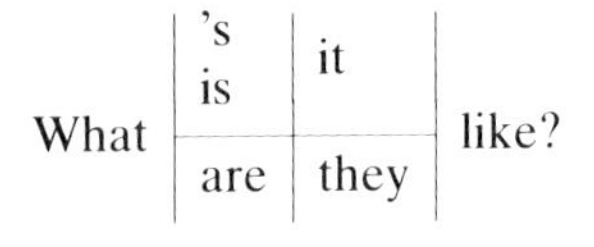

What	's is	it	like?
	are	they	

It	's is	big. expensive. fast.
They	are	blue. new.

It's big. / It's a big car. They're big. / They're big cars.
Note that adjectives in English do not agree with the following nouns.

What colour	is it?	It	's is	red / yellow / green. grey / black / white. blue / brown.
	are they?	They	're are	

What make	is it?	It	's	a Jaguar.
	are they?	They	're	Jaguars.

Ordinal numbers

1st / 2nd / 3rd / 4th / 5th / 6th / 7th / 8th

Nationalities

Italian / Swedish / German / Dutch

Expressions

Win a (Jaguar)!
What (competition)?
Fantastic!
Look at (the / this) letter.

Unit nine

Prepositions of place

It's They're She's I'm We're	in on under above below	the sea.

He's They're You're We're I'm She's	next to in front of behind	me. you. him. her. them. us.

Personal pronouns (object form): ***me, him, her*** *etc.*
Personal pronouns (subject form): ***I, he, she*** *etc.*

Put	*me* *us*	*down.*
Pull	*them* *him* *her*	*up.*

Subject pronoun – Possessive adjective – Object pronoun

I	my	me
you	your	you
she	her	her
he	his	him
we	our	us
they	their	them
it	its	it

Nationalities

-ian	an Australian the Brazilian
-an	a German the American
-ese	a Japanese the Chinese
-ish	a Spanish girl / man / person the English woman / runner
-ch	a Dutch woman / man / runner the French girl / boy / person

Unit ten

There is . . . There are . . .

Affirmative and negative

There	is isn't	a	pen	on the table. in the bag.
	are aren't	some any	pens	

Questions

Is	there	a	pen	on the table?
Are		any	pens	

Yes, there is. / No, there isn't.
Yes there are. / No, there aren't.

What's the capital of (France)?
What's the language of (Greece)?

Expressions

Stand (next to me).
Ladies and Gentlemen!
Welcome to . . .
dear
That's correct.
That's wonderful!
Here's the . . .
Well, . . .

Unit eleven

***There is** ... with uncountable nouns*
See Unit 10 for uses with countable nouns.

Affirmative and negative

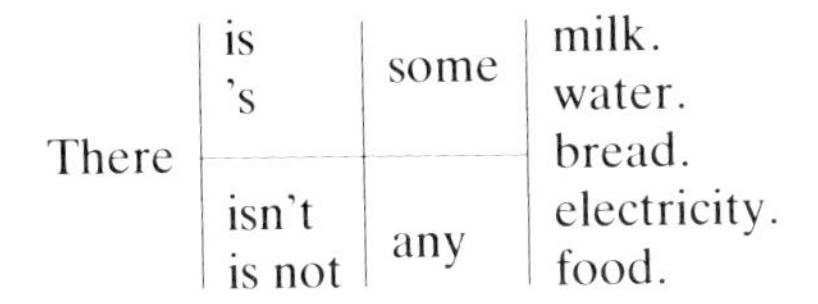

There	is 's	some	milk. water. bread. electricity. food.
	isn't is not	any	

Questions

Is	there	any	water? food?	Yes, there is. / No, there isn't.

Countable

1 – There's an orange. / There isn't a lemon.
2, 3, 4, 5 ... etc. – There are some oranges. /
There are three oranges. / There aren't any oranges.

Uncountable

There's some milk. / There isn't any milk.

Unit twelve

***Have – have got** present tense*

Affirmative

I You We They	've have	got	two sisters. some cousins. an uncle. a brother. a car.
He She	's has		

Negative

I You We They	haven't have not	got	a sister. an aunt. any cousins. any uncles.
He She	hasn't has not		

Questions

Have	you I we they	got	a brother? an aunt? a car? any sisters? any bread? a house?	Yes, (I, we) have. / No, (you, they) haven't. Yes, (she) has. / No, (he) hasn't.
Has	he she			

Possessive (genitive) of nouns
*We add **'s** to a name to show possession.*
Andrea's / Charles's

He's his brother. / He's John's brother.
It's her car. / It's Andrea's car.
They are their children. / They're John and Mary's children.
They're his pens. / They're Bill's pens.
She's his wife. / She's Charles's wife.
They're their children. / They're Amanda and Charles's children.

Note:
Words ending with an 's' or 'z' can also simply add an apostrophe (') without an extra 's' (e.g. Charles' car), but ('s) is becoming more common nowadays.

What's (your) favourite (colour)?
Who is (his) favourite (singer)?
Who are (her) favourite (singers)?

Expressions

Meet (the family).

Unit thirteen

Describing people

What	is 's	he she	like?
	are	they	

What	colour	is	his her	hair?
		are	his her	eyes?

Has	he she	got	long hair? glasses? blue eyes? a beard?
Have	you		

Describing people using the present continuous tense
*(**be** + verb **-ing** form)*

Affirmative and negative

He She	's is isn't	wearing	a jacket. blue shoes. jeans. a pullover. glasses.
I	'm 'm not		
They We You	're are aren't		suits. ties. shoes.

Questions

Am	I	wearing	a jacket? brown shoes? glasses? jeans?
Is	he she		
Are	you		
Are	we you they		ties? suits? shoes?

Expressions

Don't you know?
That's terrible!
... you know.
Really?

Unit fourteen

Asking about prices of singular, plural (countable), and uncountable things

How much	is	it? this (pen)? that (book)?
	are	they? these (pens)? those (books)?
	is	the (tea)? the (jam)?

It's £1.20.
They're 30p a pound.
They're £1.20 each.
That's £3.60 altogether.

What size (is it)?
What flavours (have you got)?

(It's / They're) **for** him / her / me / them / us / you.

Expressions

Yes, love?
Can I help you?
I'm just looking.

Unit fifteen

Imperatives

Come here!
Push!
Open the window!
Be quiet!

Don't go there.
Don't pull!
Don't open the window!
Don't be quiet!

Be	quiet! careful!

Turn on / off (the television). Turn (the television) on / off.

Turn	it the radio the light the lights them	on. off.

Help Listen to	me. him. her. us. them.

Expressions

It's no good.
Not you
Don't do that.
(That's locked), too.
What about (the back door)?

Unit sixteen

Asking for and giving directions

I'm He's She's We're You're They're	looking for	a map. a garage. the station.

Turn right / left.
Go straight on.
Go past (the church).
First right / second left.
Go along this street.
Go across the (bridge).
It's on the left / right.
It's at the end of (this street).
Take the (first left / third right).
Go straight on for about (400 metres).

Expressions

That's fine.
Is there (a bus stop) near here?
Can you tell me the way (to the Grand Hotel)?
You can't miss it.
Not at all.
I'm a stranger here.

Unit seventeen

Quantity: ***How many?***

How many	– rooms aunts	are there? have you got? has she got?	There are I've got She's got	six	. – rooms. aunts.

I haven't got any. / I haven't got any aunts. /
I've only got (two) aunts.
There aren't any. / There aren't any rooms. /
There are only (two) rooms.

I haven't got (very) many. / I haven't got (very) many books.
There aren't (very) many. / There aren't (very) many books.

Expressions

I beg your pardon?
Come in.
Pleased to meet you.
Follow me.
If you're (there), come and (see our house).
Pardon?

Unit eighteen

Asking about ownership: ***Whose?***
Possessive pronouns: ***mine, ours,*** *etc.*

Whose	– pen	is	it? this? that?	It's They're	mine. yours. his. hers. ours. theirs. Maria's.
	– pens	are	they? these? those?		

Which	one	's / is	yours? / mine? / his? / hers?	The	blue / big / new / red / small / English	one	is / 's	mine. / yours. / his. / hers.
	ones	are	ours? / Maria's?			ones	are	theirs. / Maria's.

Expressions

Come with me.
That's very kind of you.

Unit nineteen

Polite requests and offers: ***I'd like** . . . and* ***Would you like** . . .?*

I'd like (the cassette), please.

Would you like (a stamp)? | Yes, I would. / No, I wouldn't.

What / Which one / What size / Which colour / How many	would you like?

a sixty-minute cassette
a two-hour video cassette
a five-pound note (Unit 18)

Expressions

Where's it going to?
I don't know the name in English?
What's the name in English?

Unit twenty

Requests continued: ***Could we / I** . . .?* and ***I'd like** . . .*

Could	I / we	have	the menu? / a steak? / some chips?

I / We / She / He / They	'd / would	like	the menu. / a steak. / some chips.	What / How many	would	I / you / he / she / we / they	like?

Yes, (I) would.
No, (I) wouldn't.

Expressions

Sir / Madam
Is this (table) free?
(We're) in a hurry.
What about (the main course)?
And a (salad), (not chips).
It's off the menu. / It's off.
What's wrong with that?

Unit twenty-one

***Can** (present ability)*
***Can** is a modal verb, and is the same in all persons.*

After **can** *we use the infinitive without* ***to: I can drive**, etc.*

I / You / He / She / We / They	can / can't / cannot	dance. / sing. / read. / type. / drive. / run.

Can	you / I / he / she / we / they	read? / go? / type? / sing? / walk? / drive?	Yes, (I) can. / No, (she) can't.

also – He can play the guitar, and he can also play the piano.
all – We're all disabled in this group, but we can all see.

Questions

Which (languages) can you (speak)?
How many (languages) can you (speak)?
What can you do?
Who can (play the guitar)?

Unit twenty-two

Telling the time

What time / When	is	the film? / the concert?

It's	at	five / ten / a quarter / twenty / twenty-five	to / past	two.
		half past		

It's on Monday / Tuesday *etc.*

It's	in	the middle.
	at	the front. / the back. / the side.
	on	the left. / the right.

Expressions

the first / next / last performance
What would you like to see?
Where would you like to sit?
Can we have (two seats)?

Unit twenty-three

Present continuous tense (see also Unit 13):
***be** + verb **-ing** form*

He She It	's is isn't	sleeping. drinking. eating. standing.
I	'm am 'm not	sitting. reading. wearing shoes. serving dinner.
They We You	're are aren't	listening to the radio. reading a book. flying the plane.

Am	I	reading? eating? sleeping?
Is	she he it	sitting? drinking? standing?
Are	you they we	wearing shoes? serving dinner? eating dinner? drinking water? sleeping here?

Spelling:
*1. Add **-ing** to the verb: **eating**, **standing**.*
*2. Verbs ending in **e**: Take away the **e** and add **-ing**, **serve – serving**, **have – having**.*
*3. Short verbs ending in vowel – consonant: Double the consonant and add **-ing**, **sit – sitting**, **stop – stopping**.*

What (are you) doing?
What (am I) doing?
What's (she) doing?

Expressions

at the moment
Have a good (flight).
Go and look. / Go and stop her.
Is everything OK? / Is everything all right?
What's that (noise)?

Unit twenty-four

Present continuous tense with prepositions

It's moving across the sky.
They're travelling through space.
We're going towards the Earth.
She's driving away from the city.

***When** + present continuous tense*

When they're sleeping in England, they're working in Japan.

What's happening?	It's coming towards us. They're going away from the city. I'm driving across the ice. She's sleeping.

I think (my sister's working).
(My sister's working), I think.
9 o'clock in the morning / evening
3 o'clock in the afternoon
(He's) having (breakfast / lunch / dinner).
Months: January, February, etc.

Expressions

It's amazing! / It's fantastic!

Unit twenty-five

Going to** future: **be + going to + infinitive

Questions

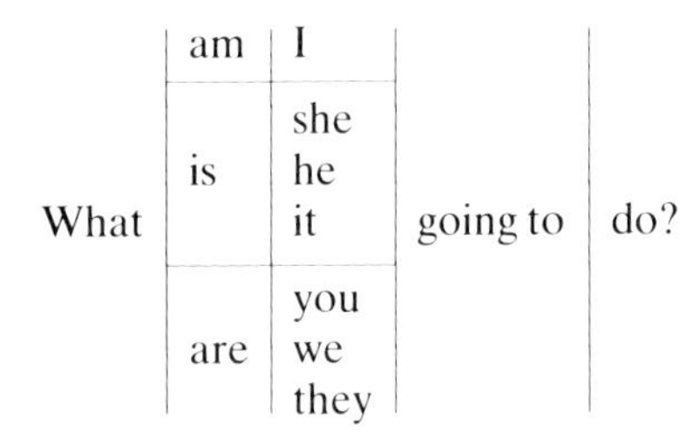

What	am	I	going to	do?
	is	she he it		
	are	you we they		

Affirmative and negative

I	'm 'm not	going to	have a sleep. open the door. be there. get into the car. telephone the police. take a photograph.
He She	's isn't		
They We You	're aren't		

Are you going to (do it), or not?
Is he going to (take it), or not?
Why?
Inside / outside / into

Expressions

Nothing's happening.
Don't tell anybody.
It's very exciting.
Wait a minute!
Quick! / Hurry!
Come on!
Calling all cars . . .
How do you do?
I'd like you to meet (my mother).
It's nice to see you again.

Unit twenty-six

***Going to** future (continued)*

Affirmative and negative

It	's isn't	going to be	hot / cold. wet / dry. sunny / cloudy. warm / cool.

It	's isn't	going to	rain. snow. thunder.

There's going to be rain / snow / thunder.

Future time words

tomorrow / next week / next month / next year / next summer / next winter

this morning / afternoon / evening

Expressions

First the bad news . . . / And the good news?
with temperatures of / about . . .
Have a nice holiday!
What's the weather like / going to be like?

Unit twenty-seven

Like, present simple tense

I We They You	like don't like	swimming. jazz. football. salad. pop music. jeans. tea. coffee.
He She	likes doesn't like	

Questions

Do	you they we I	like	swimming? jazz? football? salad? pop music? jeans? tea? coffee?	Yes, (I) do. No, (we) don't.
Does	she he			Yes, (she) does. No, (he) doesn't.

Expressions

Next question.
No way!
A box office success.
Shut up!

Unit twenty-eight

Present simple tense: ***want, need, know***

Affirmative

I You We They	want need know	that.
He She	wants needs knows	

Negative

I You We They	don't	want need know	that.
He She	doesn't		

Questions

Do Don't	you they we	want need know	that?
Does Doesn't	he she		

Offers, requests, and questions

Offers

Would you like some tea?
Do you want some tea?

Requests

I'd like some tea.
I want some tea, please.

Questions

Do you like tea?
Do you want that any more?

Expressions

I don't want this one now. / I don't want this one **any more**.
Throw it away.
. . ., then.
Anyway, . . .
That's all.

Unit twenty-nine

Present simple tense for everyday habits

I You We They	work don't work	every day. from nine to five. seven hours a day. five days a week. until six. in the mornings. on Sundays. every (Saturday).
He She	works doesn't work	

When What times Which days How many days	do you does she	work?

Frequency adverbs: ***always, sometimes, never***

I You We They	always sometimes never	have	coffee with breakfast. lunch at home. a shower in the mornings.
He She		has	

Time expressions

every week / month / year / Saturday
in the morning(s) / afternoon(s) / evening(s)
at 6 o'clock
on Sunday(s)
until 6 o'clock
from 9 to 5
for 5 hours / days / weeks / years
in three weeks
eight hours a day / seven days a week / forty weeks a year

Unit thirty

Present simple tense for everyday habits (continued)

I You	usually always	wake up get up	at	seven o'clock. seven fifteen. half past twelve. one o'clock. five thirty.
She He		has lunch comes home		

Questions with ***usually***
*(****Usually*** *is another frequency adverb.)*

What time do you usually wake up?
When does he usually have lunch?

Have *in the present simple tense*
(DO NOT use ***have got*** *in these examples.)*

Have breakfast / lunch / dinner / a shower

Unit thirty-one

Present simple tense with frequency adverbs
The adverb comes before the verb.

I You We They	always usually sometimes often	watch	TV in the evenings.
She He	hardly ever never	watches	

Be *with frequency adverbs*
The adverb comes after the verb.

It	is	always usually often sometimes hardly ever never	hot in summer cold in winter
They	are		

Questions with ***often, usually,*** *and* ***How often?***

Do	you	often usually	do it?
Does	she		

How often	do they	do it?
	does he	

It	's is	called	the outback.
They	're are		flying doctors.

I usually	go to school	by	car / train / bus / bike.
		on	foot.

Time expressions for frequency

once a week
two or three times a week
ten times a month

Expressions

... very different from
What about (doctors)?
Western Australia is **eight times the size of** Britain.
Australia is **twenty-four times the size of** Britain.

Unit thirty-two

Past simple tense of ***be: was*** *and* ***were***

Affirmative and negative

I He She It	was wasn't was not	here there	yesterday. at 3 o'clock. in the morning.
We You They	were weren't were not		

Questions

Was	I he she it	there?
Were	we you they	

Yes, (I / he / she / it) was. / No, (I / he / she / it) wasn't.
Yes, (we / you / they) were. / No, (we / you / they) weren't.

Expressions

Haven't you got any (work)?
pay day
Are you sure?
Can I borrow your (calculator)?
Poor (Tracey)

Unit thirty-three

Past simple tense of ***be****: with* ***there . . .****,* ***some****, and* ***any***

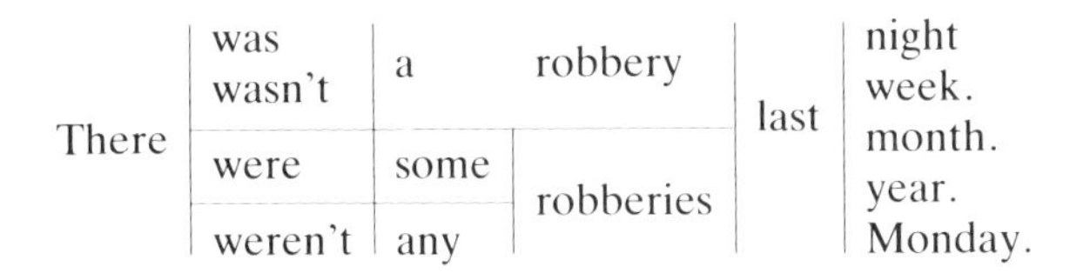

There	was wasn't	a	robbery	last	night week. month. year. Monday.
	were weren't	some any	robberies		

Was Were	there	a robbery any robberies	last	night? week? month?

Yes, there was. / No, there wasn't.
Yes, there were. / No, there weren't.

Past continuous tense ***was / were*** *+ verb +* ***-ing***

Present continuous tense: ***I am doing****.*
Past continuous tense: ***I was doing.***

I He She	was wasn't was not	wearing	a hat. glasses. a long coat.
We You They	were weren't were not		hats. long coats. glasses.

What was (she) wearing?
What were (they) wearing?

Expressions

Beware of (pickpockets).
Remember this (face).
It's impossible! / It's not impossible.

Unit thirty-four

Past simple tense: irregular verbs
Many of the most frequent verbs are 'irregular' in the past. You will need to learn them.

Affirmative and negative

I You He She We They	went didn't go did not go	to the supermarket to the bank there	yesterday. last Saturday. last night.

Questions

Did Didn't	you I he she we they	go	there	yesterday? last week? last month? last night? last year? at 9 o'clock?

Yes, (I) did. / No, (she) didn't.

When did you go there?	I went there yesterday.
What did he buy?	He bought some chicken.
What did they get?	They got some beef.
What did we have?	We had a cup of tea.
What did you do?	I went home.

Note
Present simple: ***I don't do it****. Past simple:* ***I didn't do it.***
Present simple question: ***Do you do it?*** *Past simple question:* ***Did you do it?***
You can always make negative sentences and questions in the past if you know the present form of the verb: you simply change ***do / does*** *to* ***did****.*

Expressions

Can I ask you a few questions?
Can you get it, please?
They all (bought meat at Safebury's).
Well, that's all right, then.
Great!
Let's go home.

Unit thirty-five

Past simple tense: irregular verbs (continued)
Indefinite pronouns: ***something / anything, someone / anyone***

Affirmative

I He She You We They	saw heard	something. someone.

Negative

I He She You We They	didn't did not	see hear	anyone. anything.

Questions

Did Didn't	I you he she we they	see hear	anyone? anything?

Yes, (I) did. / No, (she) didn't.

Did you find a telephone?
I didn't find a telephone. I found a hotel.

Did you say anything?
I didn't say anything. / I said 'Be quiet!'

Did she put it on the bed?
She didn't put it on the bed. / She put it on the table.

Affirmative: ***some, someone, something.***
Negative and questions: ***any, anyone, anything.***

Expressions

It's freezing!
I'm frightened.
You wait here.
What do you think?
What's the matter?
(He was) like (Count Dracula).
Don't be silly.
This isn't funny.

Unit thirty-six

Past simple tense: regular verbs

add ***-d***	*add* ***-ed***
live / lived	want / wanted
move / moved	look / looked
fire / fired	visit / visted
score / scored	kill / killed
die / died	ask / asked
arrive / arrived	sail / sailed
love / loved	weigh / weighed

-y *to* ***-ied***	*double the letter*
marry / married	stop / stopped
worry / worried	slip / slipped
hurry / hurried	travel / travelled

What happened?	He scored two goals for Scotland. He killed three horses. He slipped off and landed in the river.

Sequence adverbs with the past tense: ***First . . . then . . . finally***

Expressions

He fired his gun six times.
He lived from 1413 to 1452.
They sailed round the world three times between 1646 and 1657.

Unit thirty-seven

Tag questions: ***– isn't it? / – is it?***

It	's is	a very nice day, an awful day, a cold day,	isn't it?

It	isn't is not	very nice, very warm, cold,	is it?

You They	sound	friendly. unhappy. angry.

-ing form

I you we they	like enjoy	reading. collecting things. swimming. doing aerobics. playing football.
He she	likes enjoys	

We (do / did) some (writing / reading).

Past tenses
come – came   take – took

Expressions

It's very warm . . . for Spring.
But not always.
'Morning.
What kind of (books do you like)?
That's wonderful. / That's nice.

Unit thirty-eight

Will *for future simple*

Affirmative and negative

I You He She We They	'll will won't will not	be (there) do it	tomorrow. soon. on Sunday. next (week).

Questions

Will	I you he she we they	be there? do it?

Yes, (I) will. / No, (we) won't.

What time will (she) be there?
When will (they) do it?

Will *has many uses in English, and future reference is only one of them.*

Dates

August 3rd (August the third, the third of August)

Expressions

Look at the time!
Don't worry.
on time
Here it comes now.
Thank goodness for that!

Unit thirty-nine

***Will** and **shall** for offers and suggestions*

Offers

Offer	*Accepting*	*Refusing*
I'll do it. Shall I do it?	Yes, please. Thank you very much. That's very kind of you. That's very nice of you.	No, thank you. No, it's all right. I'll do it. Thank you, but I can do it. That's very kind, but no thanks.

Suggestions

Shall we Let's Why don't we	go out(?) go to a party(?) see some friends(?)

Where shall we go?
What shall we do?
Who shall we go and see?

***Want to do (want + to** infinitive)*

I	want don't want wanted didn't want	to	do it. go out. cross the road. be late.

Expressions

That's very nice of you.
There you are.
I've got (a headache / a temperature).
That's too expensive.
That's a good idea.
I don't want to.

Unit forty

Each	player throws the dice. space has a number.

When you pass over a red space, read the instruction.

If you finish on a red space, read the instruction.

Acknowledgements

We would like to thank everyone involved in producing, piloting, and designing *Grapevine* 1 for their efforts and inspiration.
We would particularly like to thank our editors David Wilson (Student's Book, Teacher's Book, Workbooks) and Tim Blakey (Video Activity Book), together with Michael Daniell, Simon Murison-Bowie, Cristina Whitecross, and Suzanna Harsanyi for their editorial support and encouragement.
On the art and design side of the Student's Book, Teacher's Book, and Workbooks, we would like to thank the designer, Pearl Bevan, her team (E. Mitchell, L. Darroux, J. Hill), and the art editor, Katy Wheeler. For the design of the Video Activity Book, our thanks go to Phil Hall. We are grateful to Malcolm Price for handling the production of all components.
Our thanks are also due to the team of actors and technical crew who brought the video to life, and particularly to our producer, Rob Maidment, and director, Bob Speirs.
For the audio cassettes, we are grateful to James Richardson (Producer) and Vince Cross (music).
We would like to add our thanks to the Oxford University Press ELT representatives around the world, for their help, insights, and friendship during the last ten years.

The authors and publishers are grateful to the following institutions and their staff for piloting *Grapevine* and for providing invaluable comment and feedback:

LinguaSec, Madrid, Spain; Cambridge English Studies, La Coruña, Spain; I.B. Fernando Herrera, Sevilla, Spain; Teach In Language and Training Workshop SRL, Rome, Italy; Oxford School of English SRL, Udine, Italy; Four Seasons Language School, Hamamatsu, Japan; Alec School of Languages, Tokyo, Japan; Shizuoka Seika Gakuen, Shizuoka, Japan; Sociedade Brasileira de Cultura Inglesa, Belo Horizonte, Brazil; Colegio Ward, Ramos Mejia, Pcia. de Buenos Aires, Argentina; Riyadh Language Institute, Riyadh, Saudi Arabia; Lanis Language School, Volos, Greece; Marinou Language School, Athens, Greece; Stamatopoulou Language School, Athens, Greece.

The publishers would like to thank the following for their permission to reproduce photographs:

Ace Photo Agency/Mike Bluestone, Gabe Palmer, Diane Miller 12
Allsport/Simon Brut 9; David Cannon, Tony Duffy, Bob Martin, Don Smith 12
Austin Rover 3
Barnaby's Picture Library 37
David Cannon 12
John Cleare Mountain Camera 37
Colorsport - Introduction, 37
Compix 31
Greg Evans Photo Library 3, 37
The Image Bank/Derek Berwin, Kay Charnush, Gary Cralle, Brett Froomer, Larry Gatz, Garry Gay, Antonio Rosario, Steve Schatzberg, M Tchereukoff, Trevor Wood, - Introduction, Unit 3; Cliff Feulner, Ted Kawalerski, Elyse Lewin, Christa Peters, 12; Steve Krongard 31
Jaguar Cars 8
Luton & District Transport 3
Adrian Meredith - Introduction, 3, 5
NEFF (UK) Ltd 8
Philips 8
Photographers Library 38
Rex Features Ltd/John Rogers 12
Seat 8
Sony (UK) Ltd 8, 19
Viewfinder - Introduction, 3, 38
Volvo 8
Waterski International, Joe McCarthy 8
Zanussi Ltd 8

and the following for their time and assistance:

Science Studio, Oxford
Levi Strauss UK
Sylvesters, Oxford

The publishers would also like to thank Guinness Publishing Limited for permission to credit adapted information (in Unit 21) to *The Guinness Book of Records* © Guinness Publishing Limited 1988.

Illustrations by:

John Bendall 6
Manuel Benet/Bardon Press SFP 1
Peter Elson/Sarah Brown Agency 24
Elitta Fell SFP 1
Phil Gascoine 9
Robina Green 11, 24, 39
Paul Hampson/Funny Business 34
Tina Hancocks/John Martin Artists 11
Jim Hodgson 3, 14, 18
Stephen Holmes 40
Ian Kellas/Funny Business 15, 20, 21, 23, 25, 38, SFP 3
Pat Ludlow/Linda Rogers Associates 21
Rolf Mohr/Sarah Brown Agency 7
Mike Ogden SFP 4
Oxford Illustrators 8, 9, 16, 26, 31
Colin Paine 27
Joanna Quinn 37, 39
John Richardson/Funny Business 29
Chris Riddell 1, 16, 17, 28, 36
Anthony Sidwell 16
Kate Simpson 2, 13, SFP 2
Jane Smith cover
Kay Smith 19
Brian Walker 4, 33

Studio and location photographs by:

Rob Judges, Mark Mason, Franta Provaznik

Stills photography by Rob Judges

Oxford University Press
Walton Street, Oxford OX2 6DP

Oxford New York Toronto
Delhi Bombay Calcutta Madras Karachi
Petaling Jaya Singapore Hong Kong Tokyo
Nairobi Dar es Salaam Cape Town
Melbourne Auckland

and associated companies in
Berlin Ibadan

OXFORD and Oxford English
are trade marks of Oxford University Press

First published 1989
Third impression 1990

ISBN 0 19 425381 3 Student's Book

ISBN 0 19 425382 1 Teacher's Book

ISBN 0 19 425383 X Workbook (part A)

ISBN 0 19 425385 6 Workbook (part B)

ISBN 0 19 425384 8 Audio cassettes (x 2)

Video – VHS PAL (other formats available)

ISBN 0 19 458375 9 Video cassette 1

ISBN 0 19 458384 8 Video cassette 2

ISBN 0 19 458393 7 Video Activity Book

Printed in Hong Kong